DRAW EDWARD!

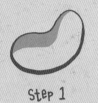

Step 1

Step 2

Step 3

Step 4

Sleeping

Walking

Trotting

Running (fast!)

Sweet dance moves

Play time

Snack time

Party time

Content

Angry

Surprised

Space explorer

Hocus Focus

James Sturm
Andrew Arnold
Alexis Frederick-Frost

First Second
New York

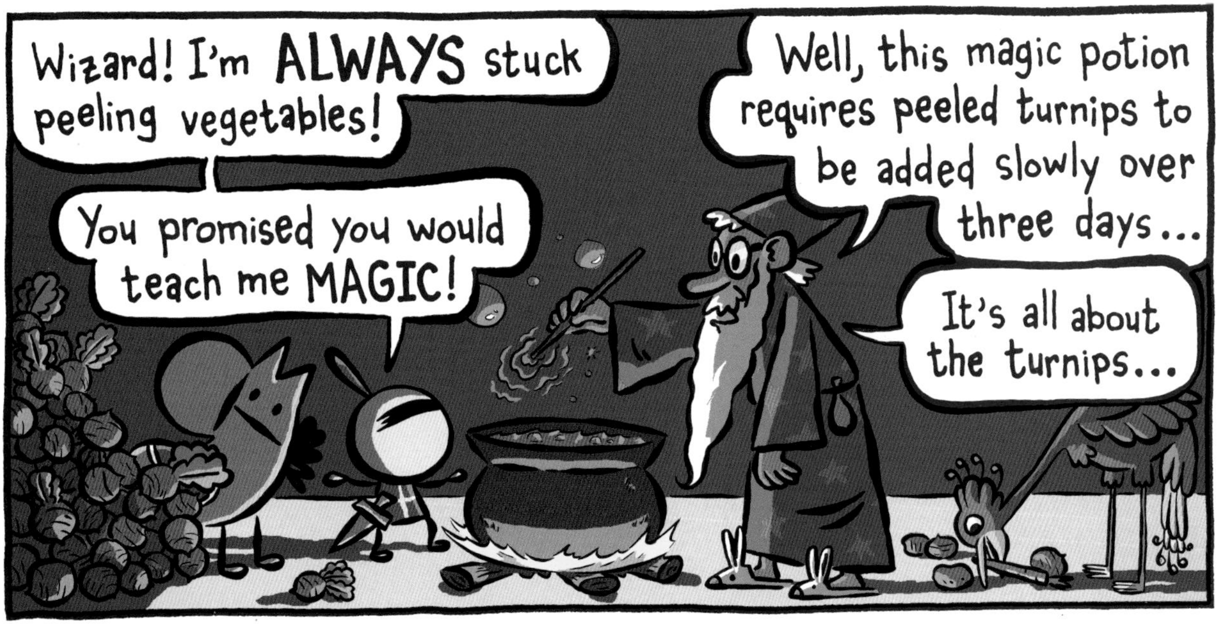
Wizard! I'm ALWAYS stuck peeling vegetables!
You promised you would teach me MAGIC!
Well, this magic potion requires peeled turnips to be added slowly over three days...
It's all about the turnips...

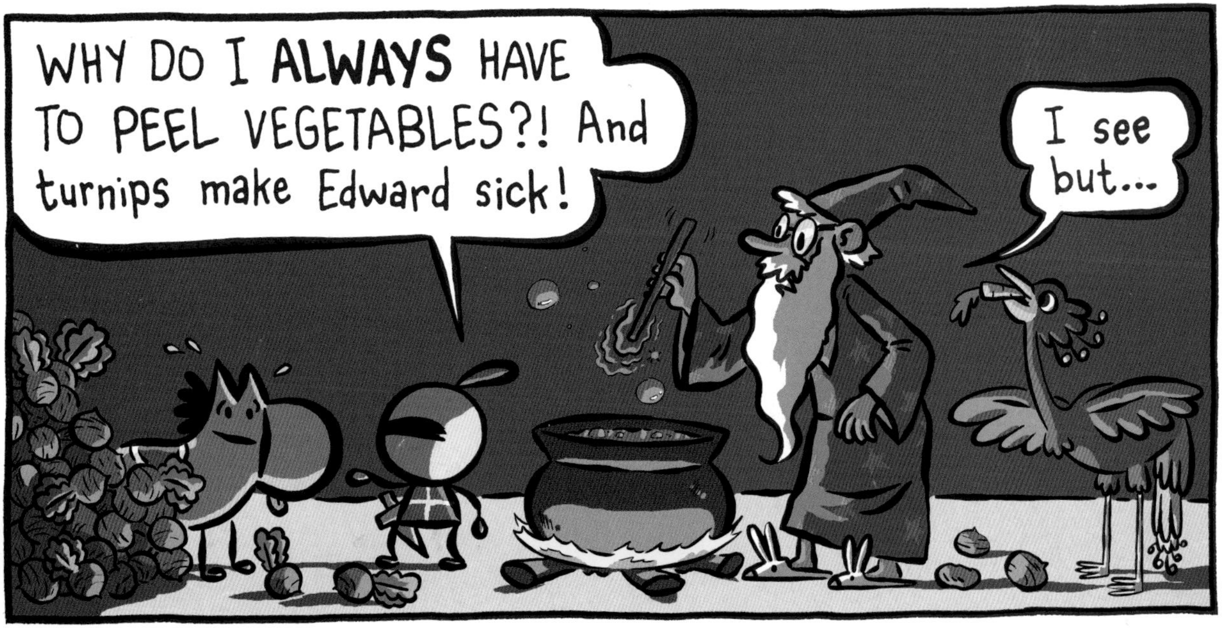
WHY DO I ALWAYS HAVE TO PEEL VEGETABLES?! And turnips make Edward sick!
I see but...

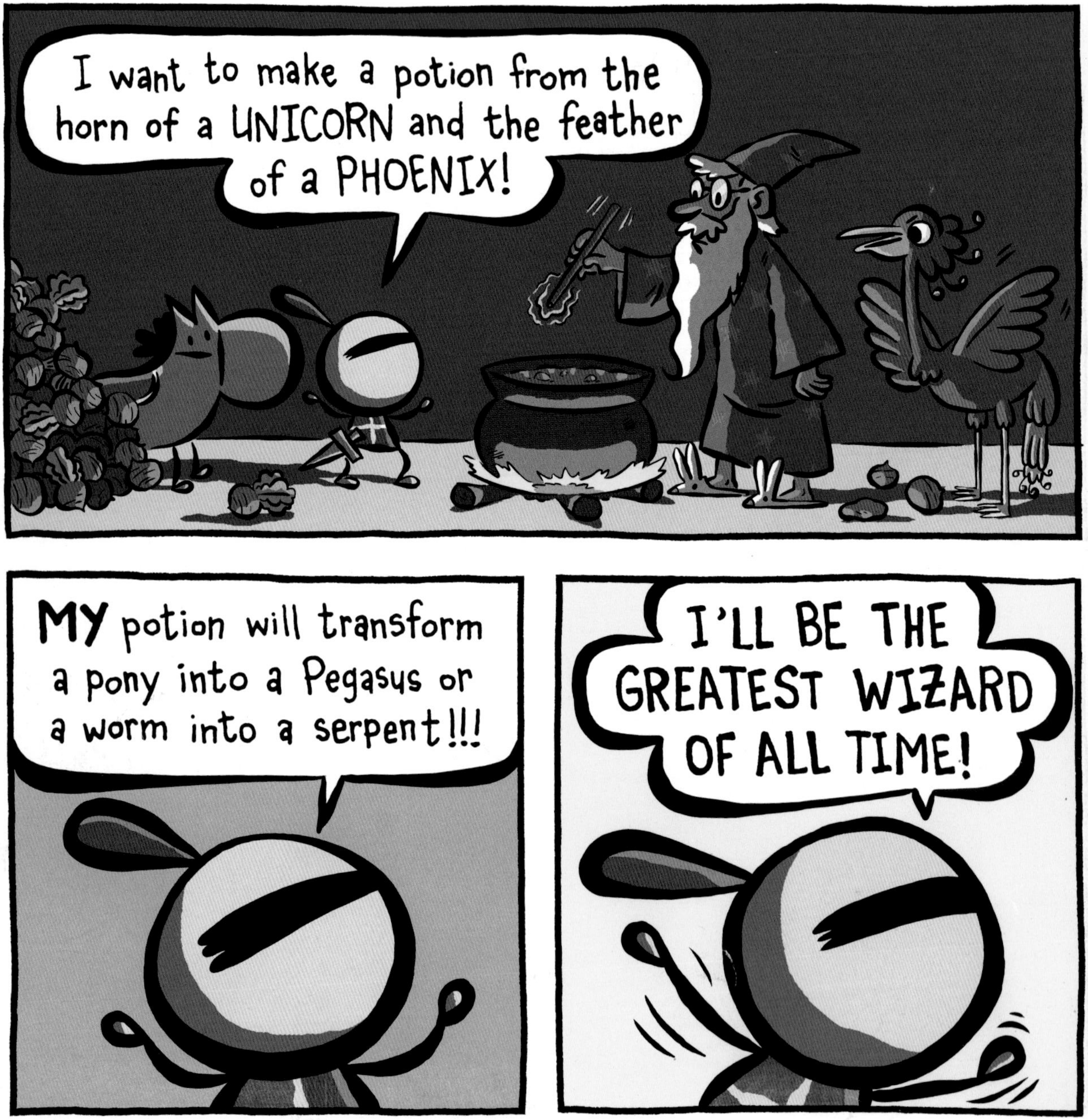
I want to make a potion from the horn of a UNICORN and the feather of a PHOENIX!
MY potion will transform a pony into a Pegasus or a worm into a serpent!!!
I'LL BE THE GREATEST WIZARD OF ALL TIME!

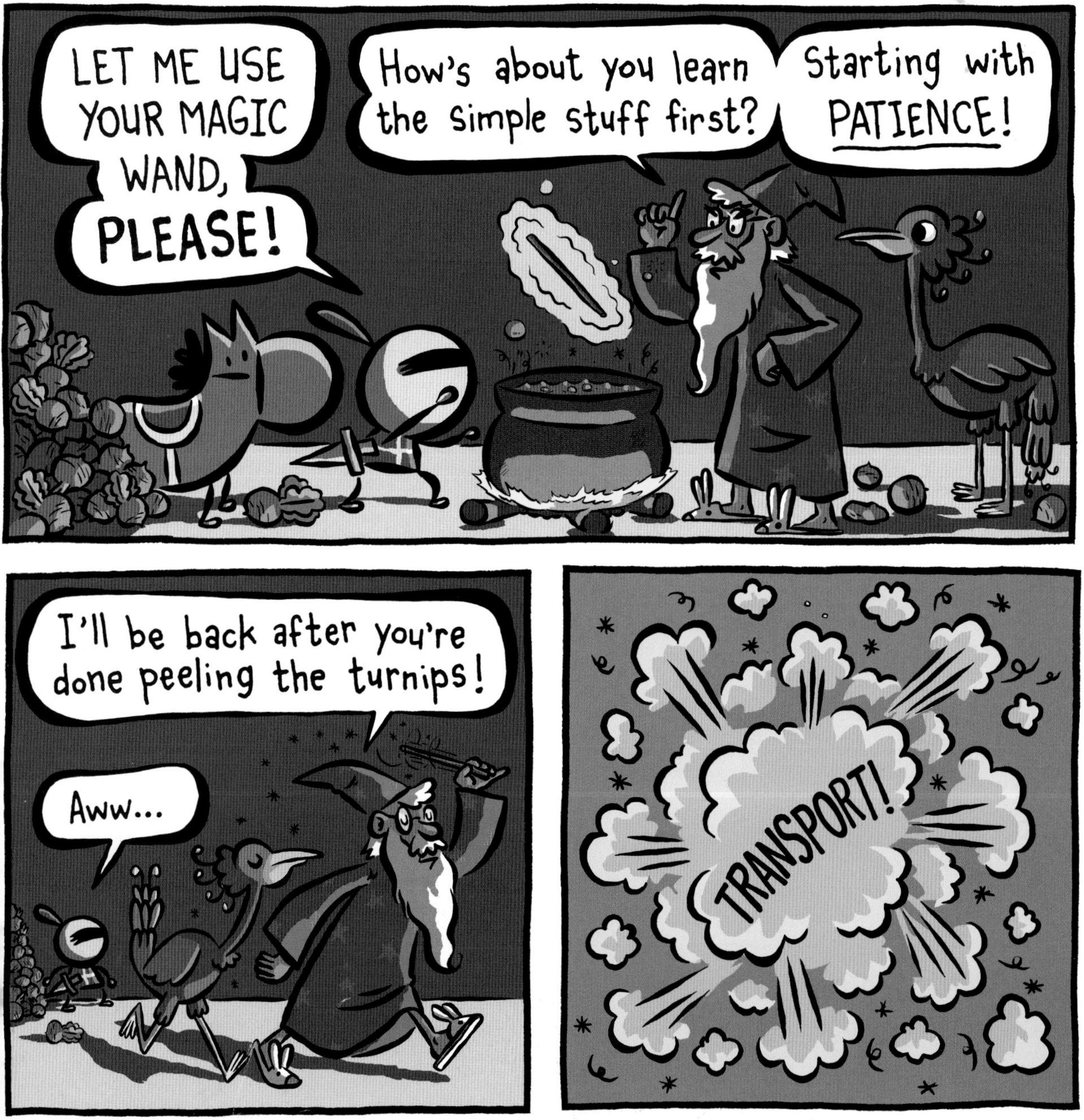
LET ME USE YOUR MAGIC WAND, PLEASE!
How's about you learn the simple stuff first?
Starting with PATIENCE!
I'll be back after you're done peeling the turnips!
Aww...
TRANSPORT!

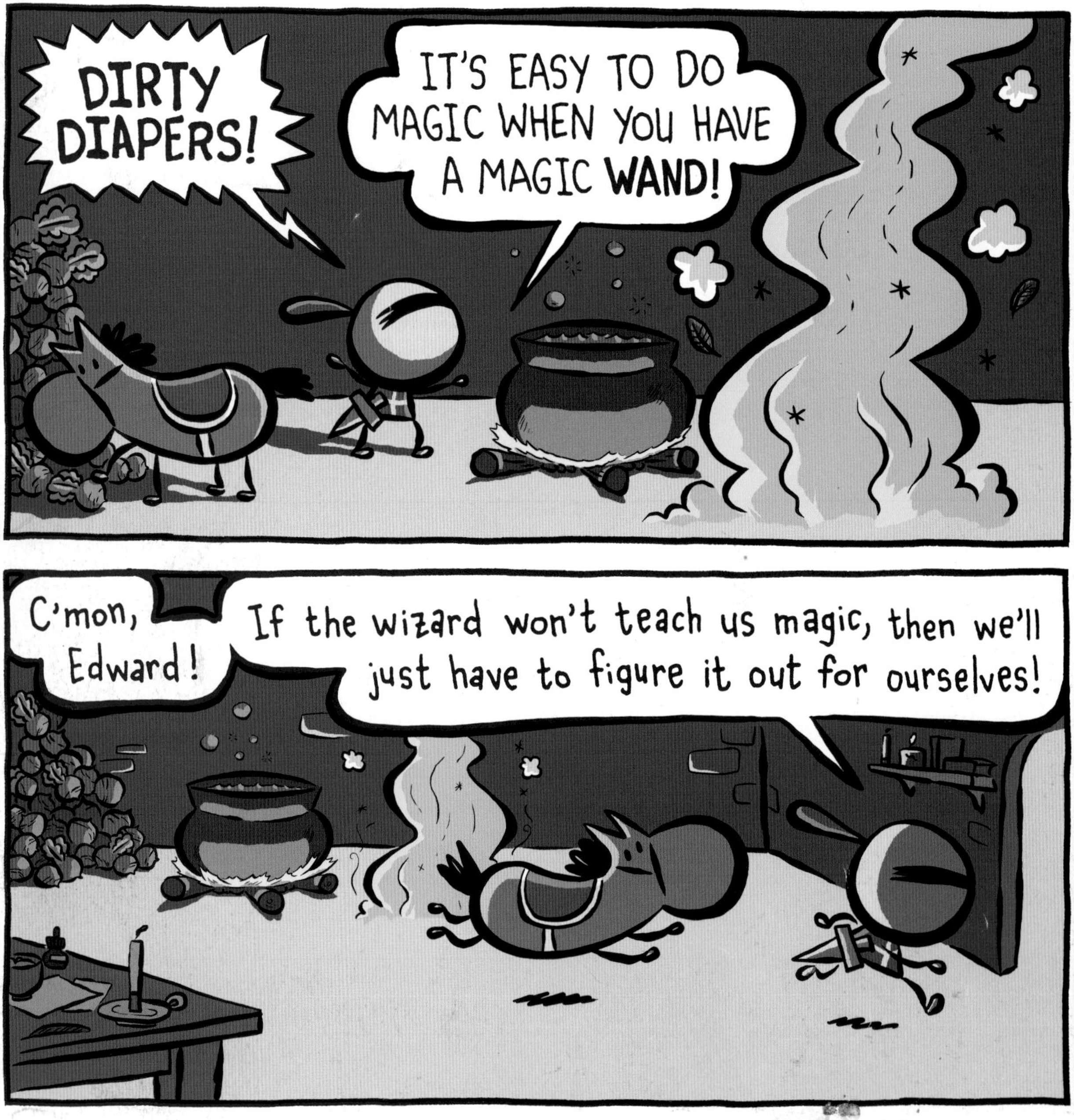
DIRTY DIAPERS!
IT'S EASY TO DO MAGIC WHEN YOU HAVE A MAGIC **WAND**!
C'mon, Edward!
If the wizard won't teach us magic, then we'll just have to figure it out for ourselves!

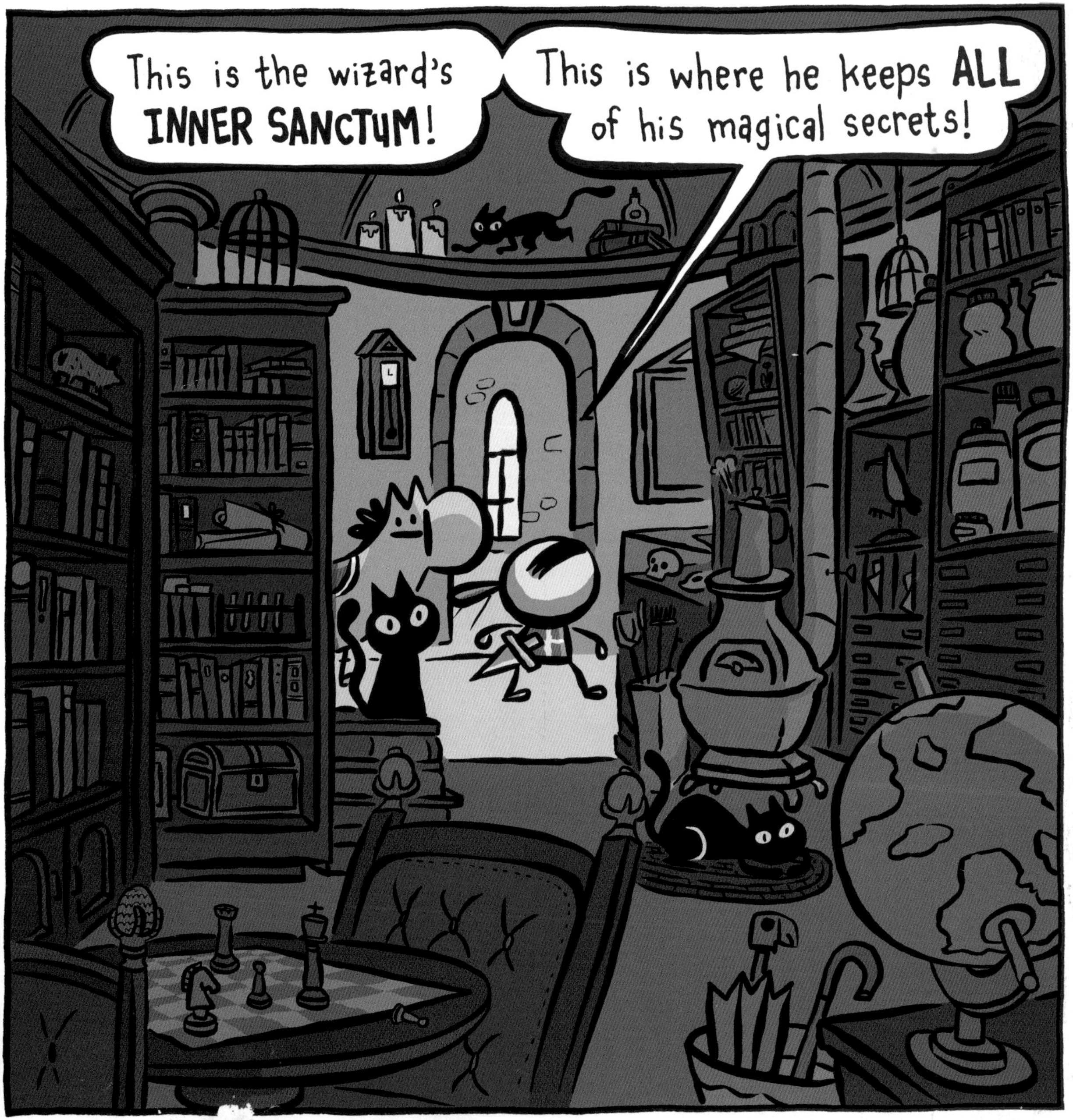
This is the wizard's INNER SANCTUM!
This is where he keeps ALL of his magical secrets!

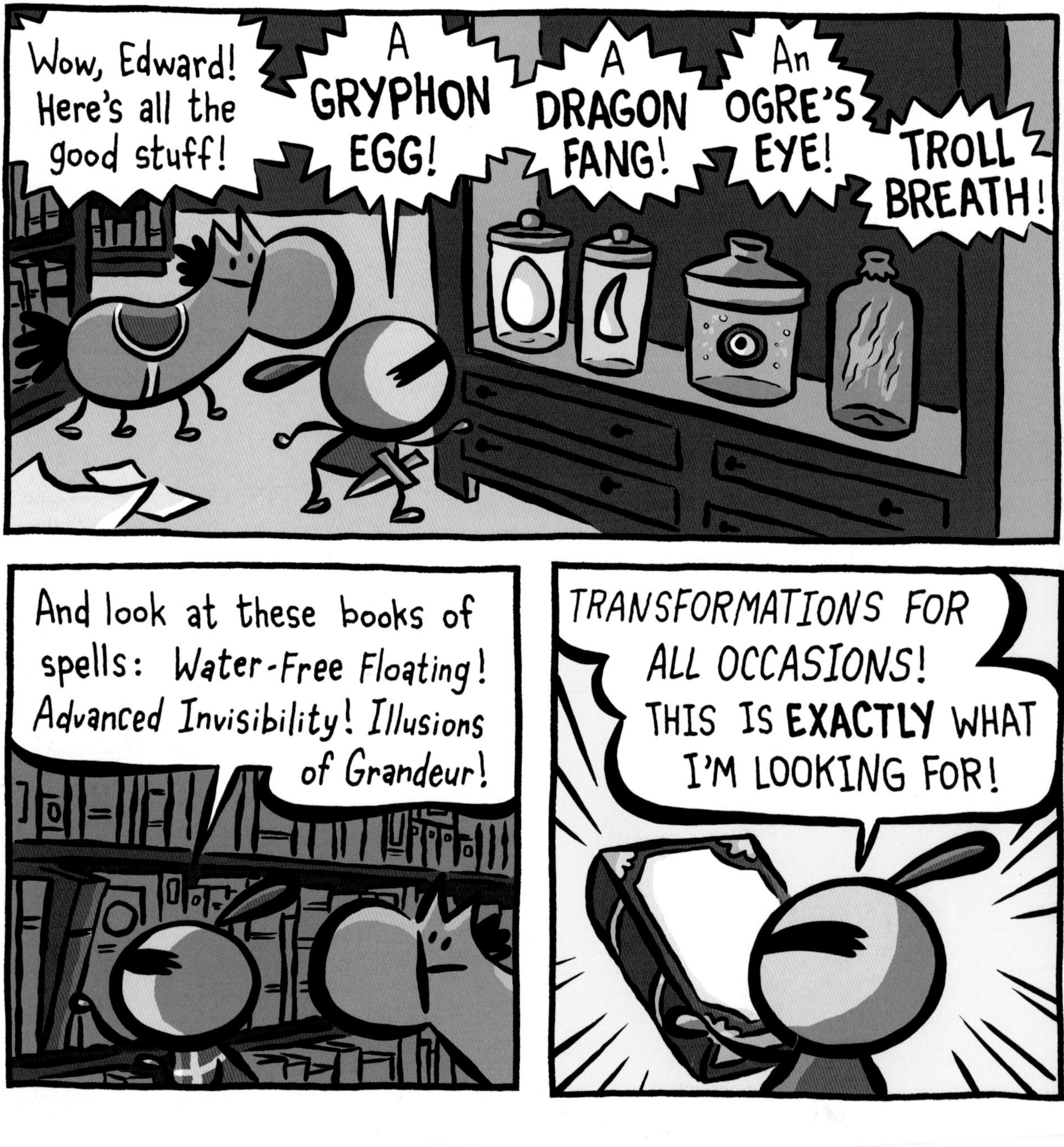
Wow, Edward! Here's all the good stuff!
A GRYPHON EGG!
A DRAGON FANG!
An OGRE'S EYE!
TROLL BREATH!
And look at these books of spells: Water-Free Floating! Advanced Invisibility! Illusions of Grandeur!
TRANSFORMATIONS FOR ALL OCCASIONS! THIS IS EXACTLY WHAT I'M LOOKING FOR!

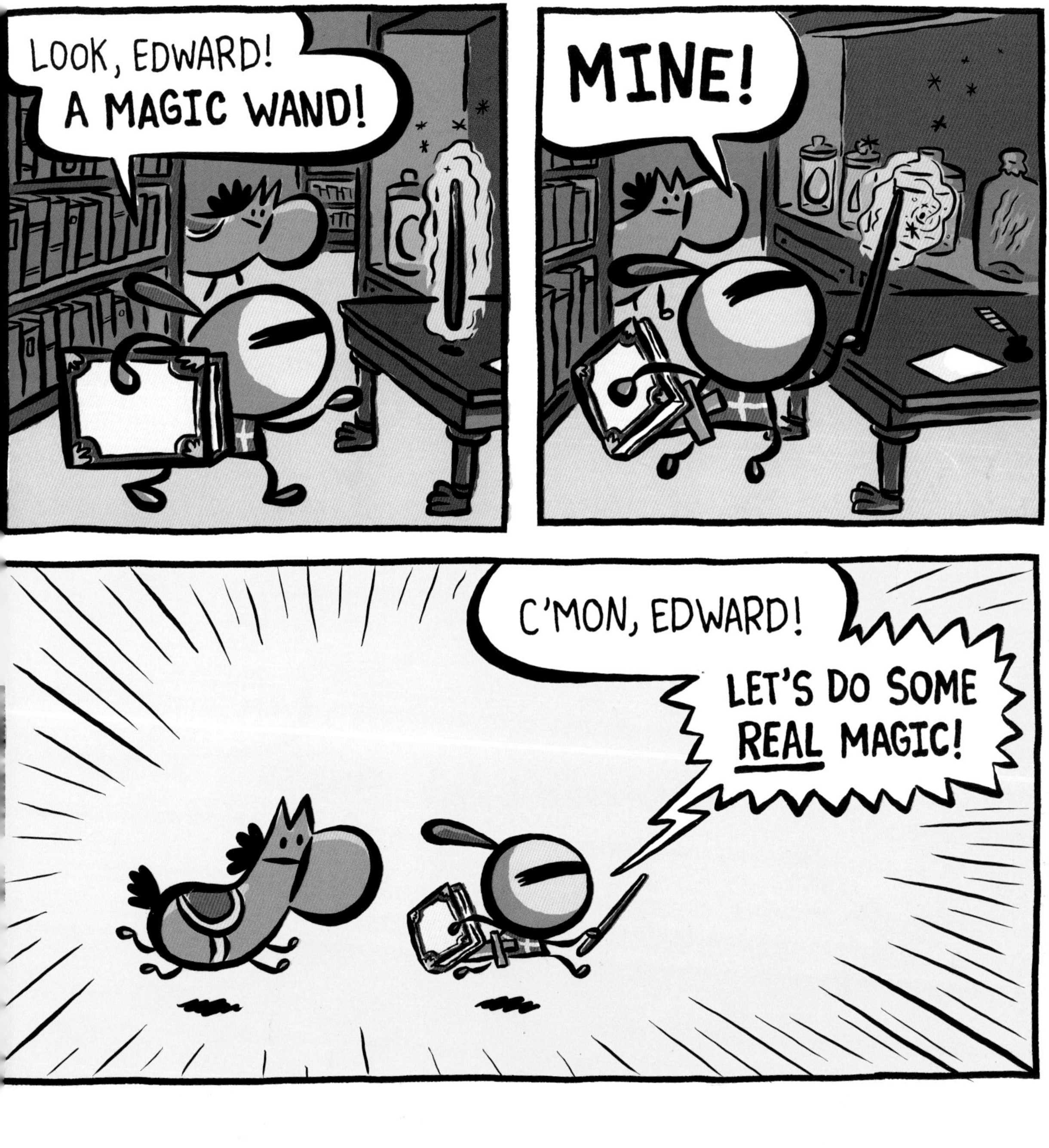
LOOK, EDWARD! A MAGIC WAND!
MINE!
C'MON, EDWARD!
LET'S DO SOME REAL MAGIC!

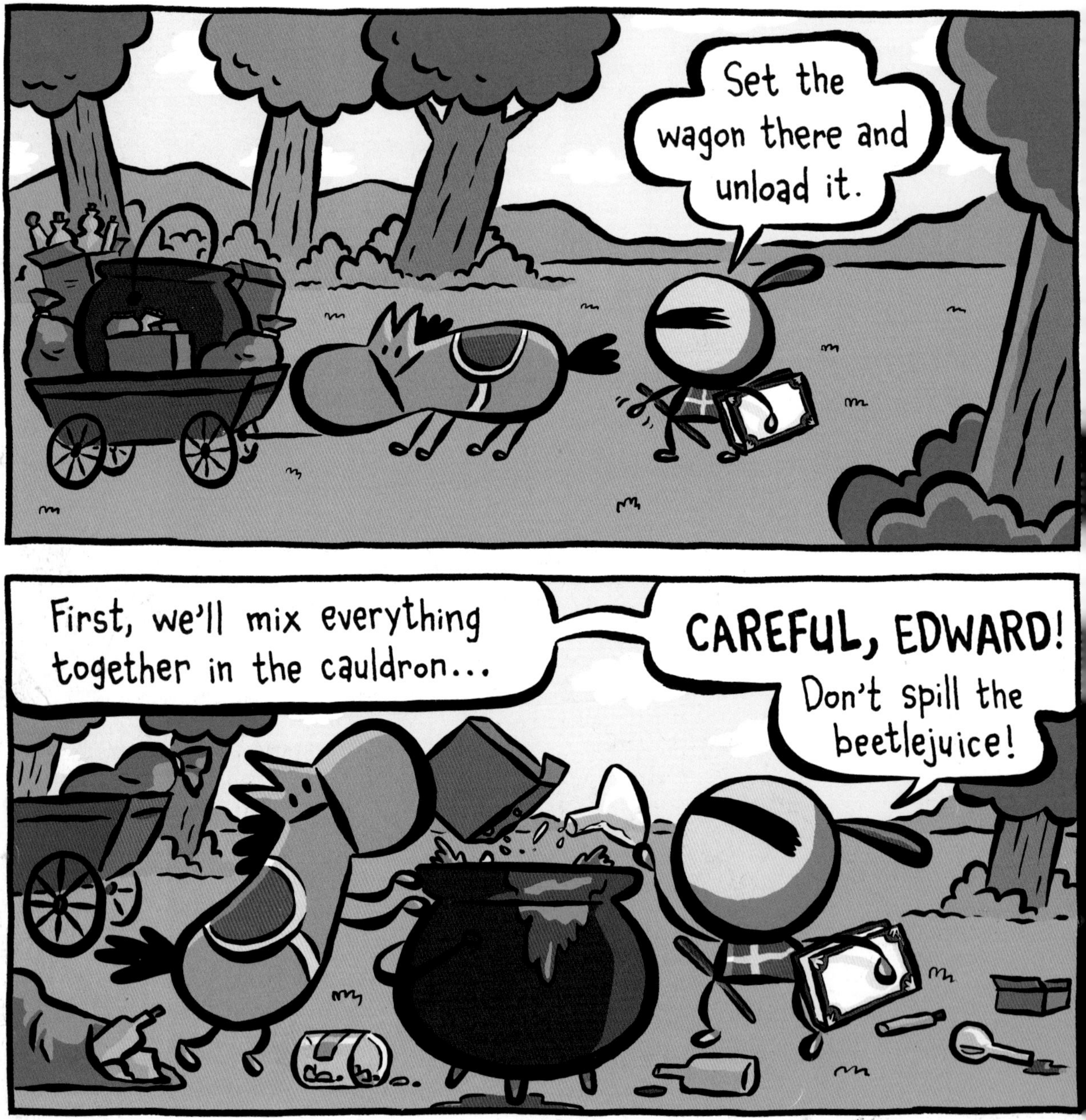
Set the wagon there and unload it.
First, we'll mix everything together in the cauldron...
CAREFUL, EDWARD! Don't spill the beetlejuice!

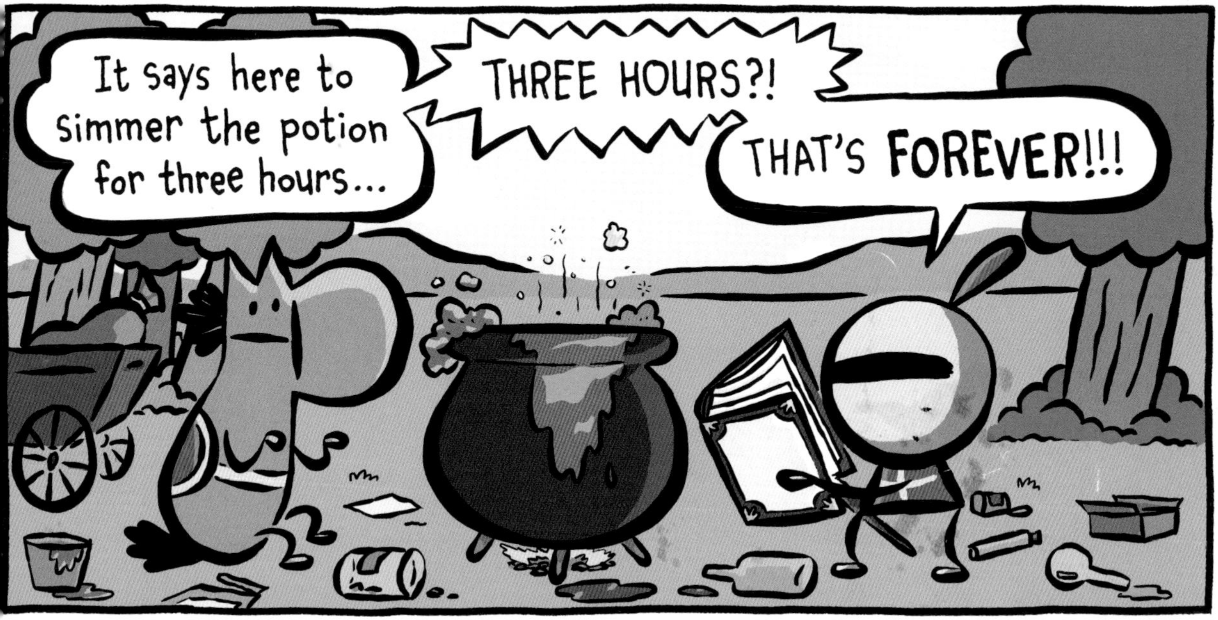
It says here to simmer the potion for three hours...
THREE HOURS?!
THAT'S **FOREVER!!!**

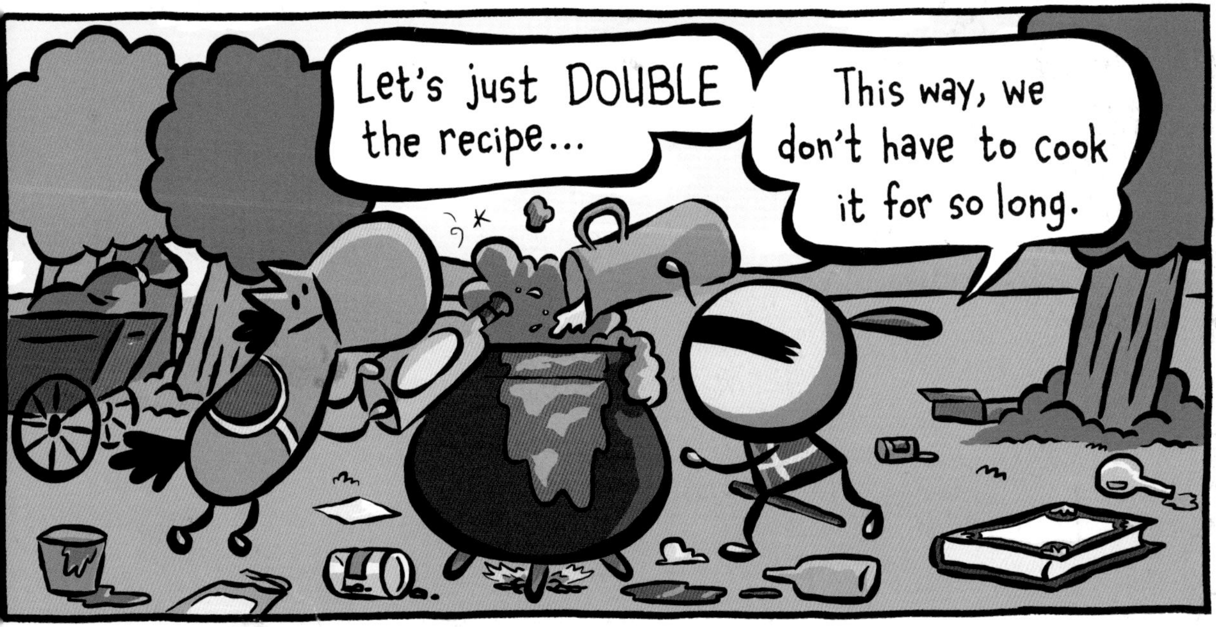
Let's just DOUBLE the recipe...
This way, we don't have to cook it for so long.

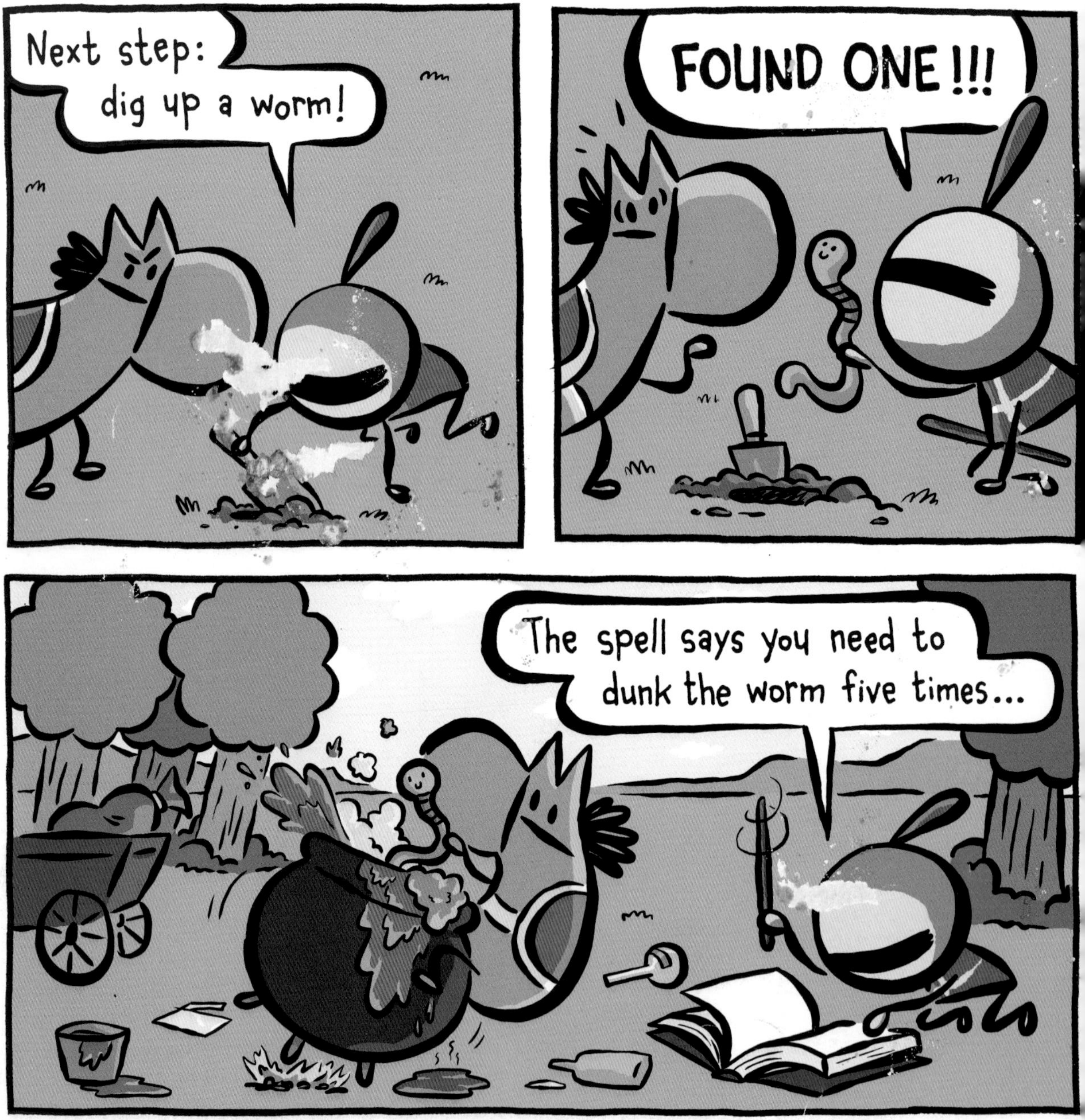
Next step: dig up a worm!
FOUND ONE!!!
The spell says you need to dunk the worm five times...

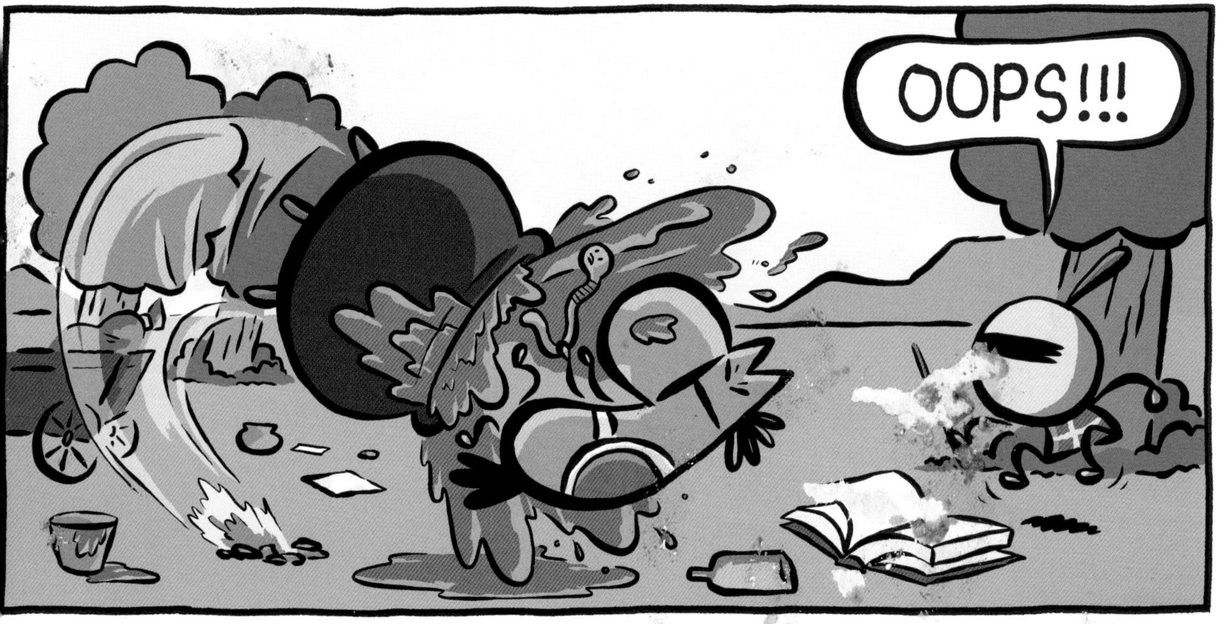
OOPS!!!

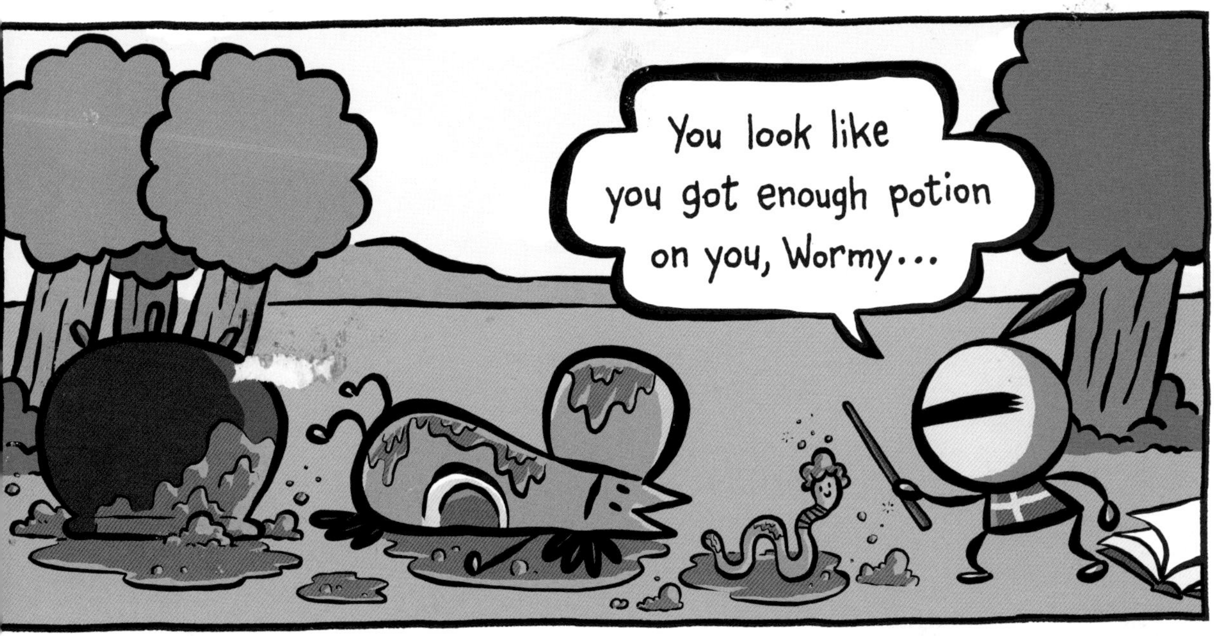
You look like you got enough potion on you, Wormy...

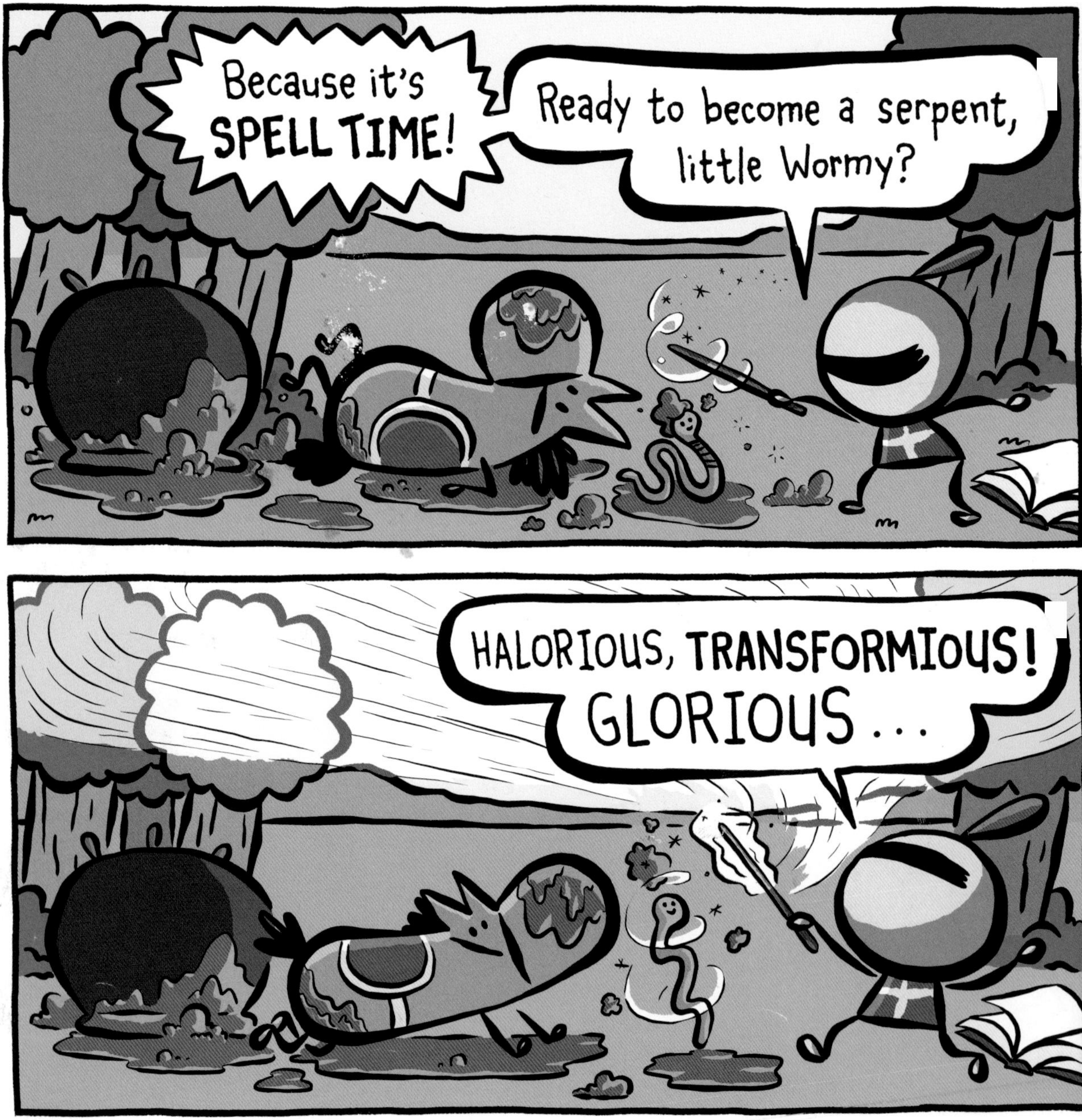

Because it's SPELL TIME!
Ready to become a serpent, little Wormy?
HALORIOUS, TRANSFORMIOUS! GLORIOUS . . .

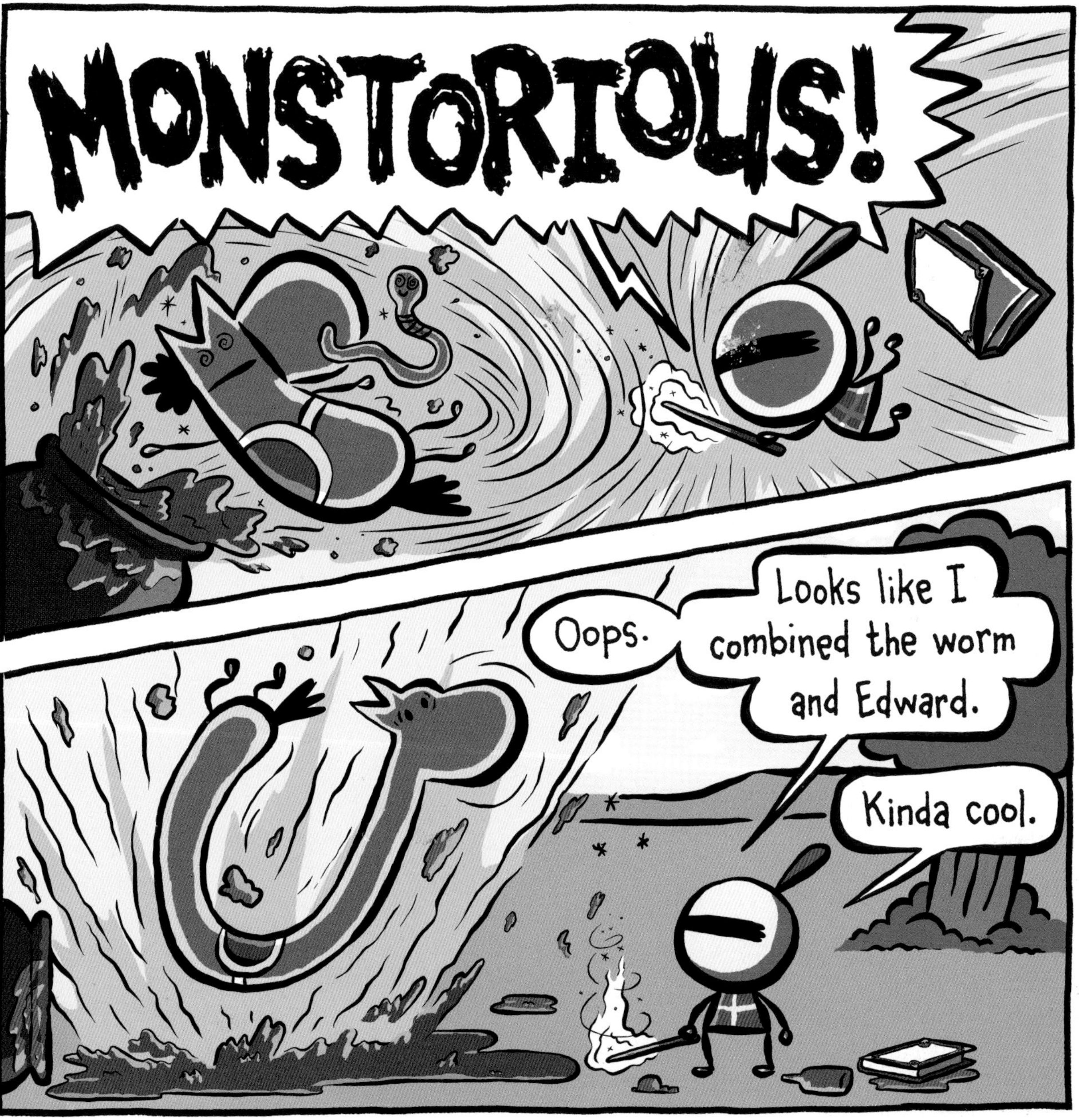
MONSTORIOUS!
Oops.
Looks like I combined the worm and Edward.
Kinda cool.

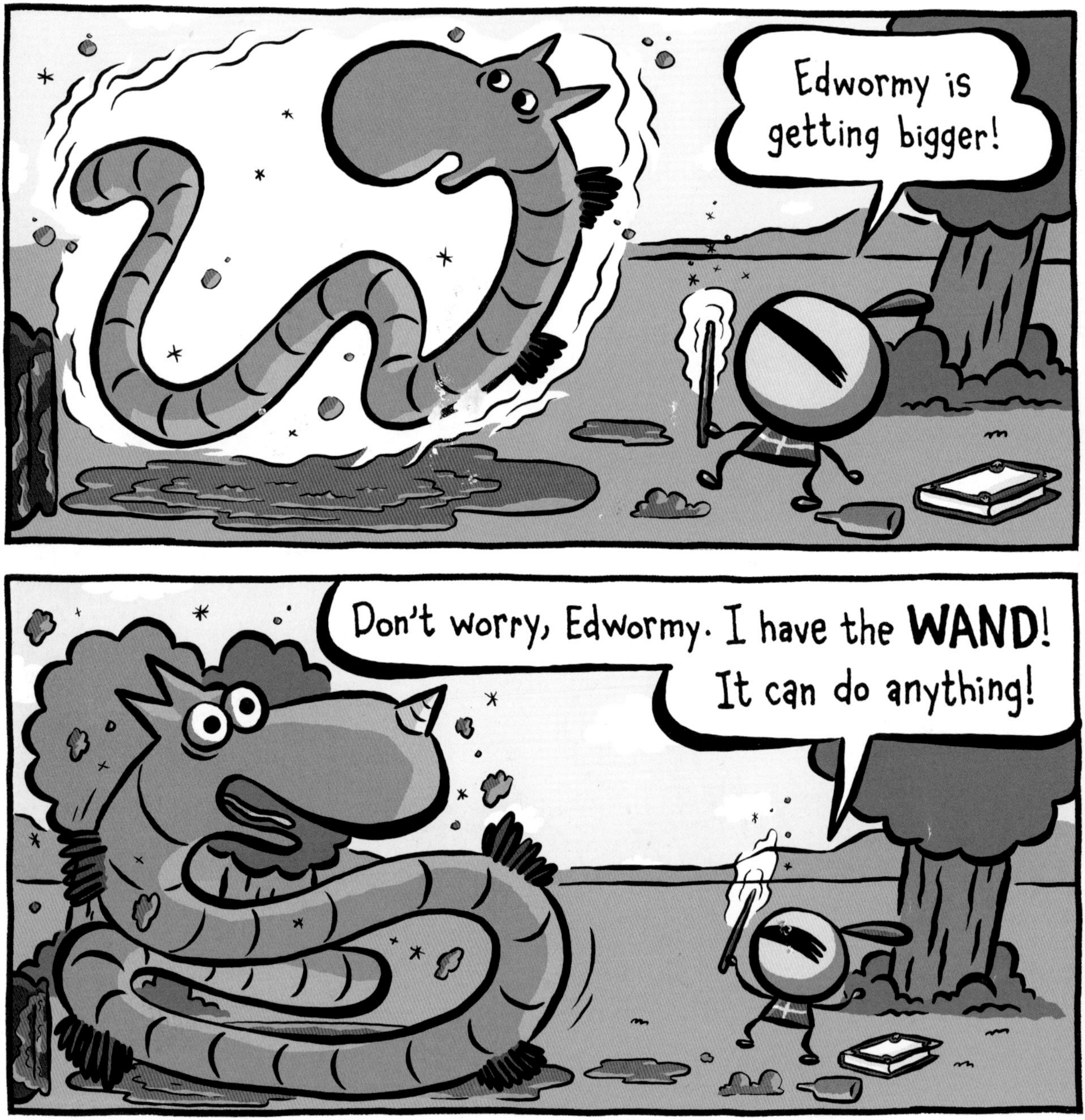
Edwormy is getting bigger!
Don't worry, Edwormy. I have the WAND! It can do anything!

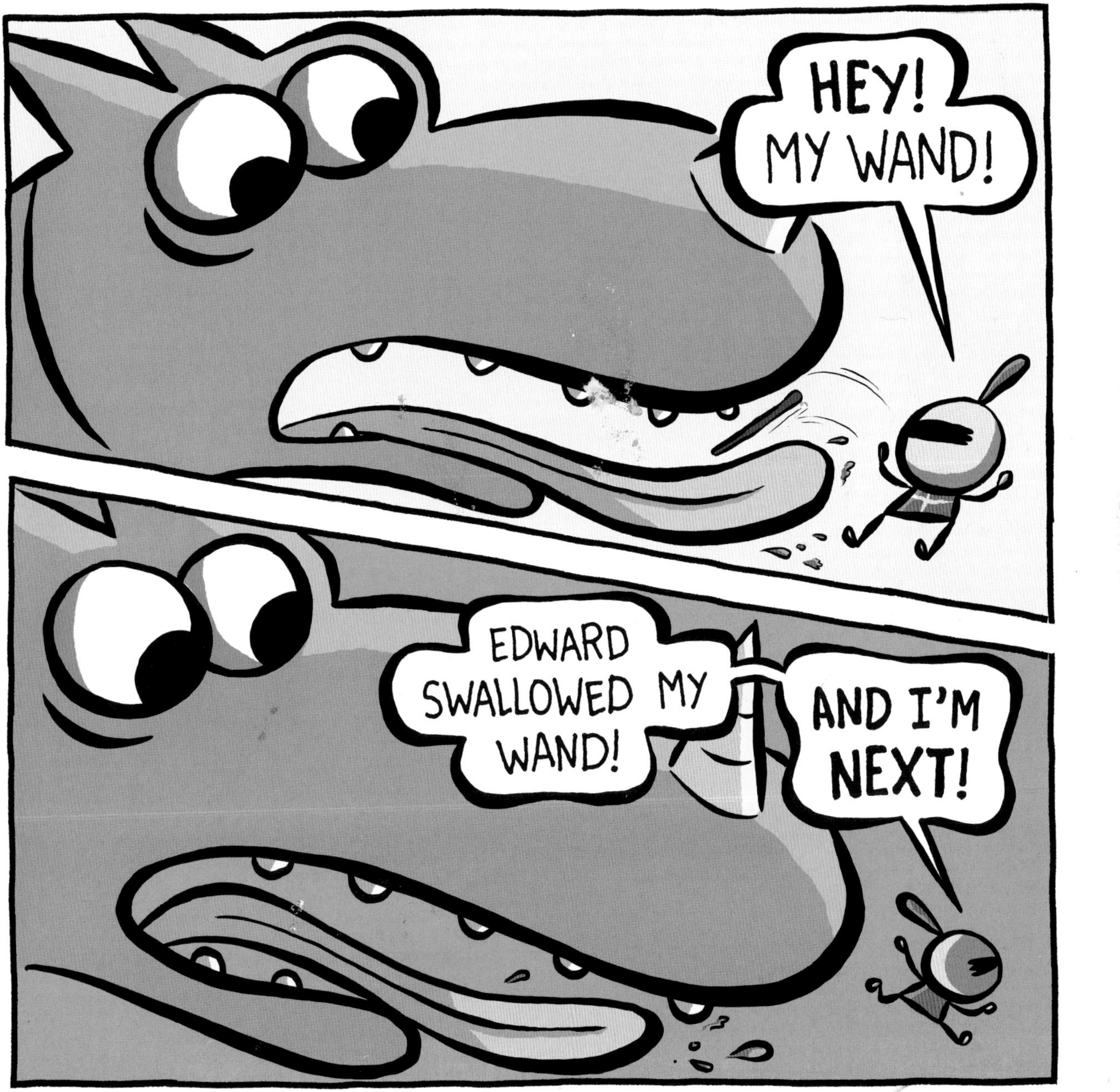
HEY! MY WAND!
EDWARD SWALLOWED MY WAND!
AND I'M NEXT!

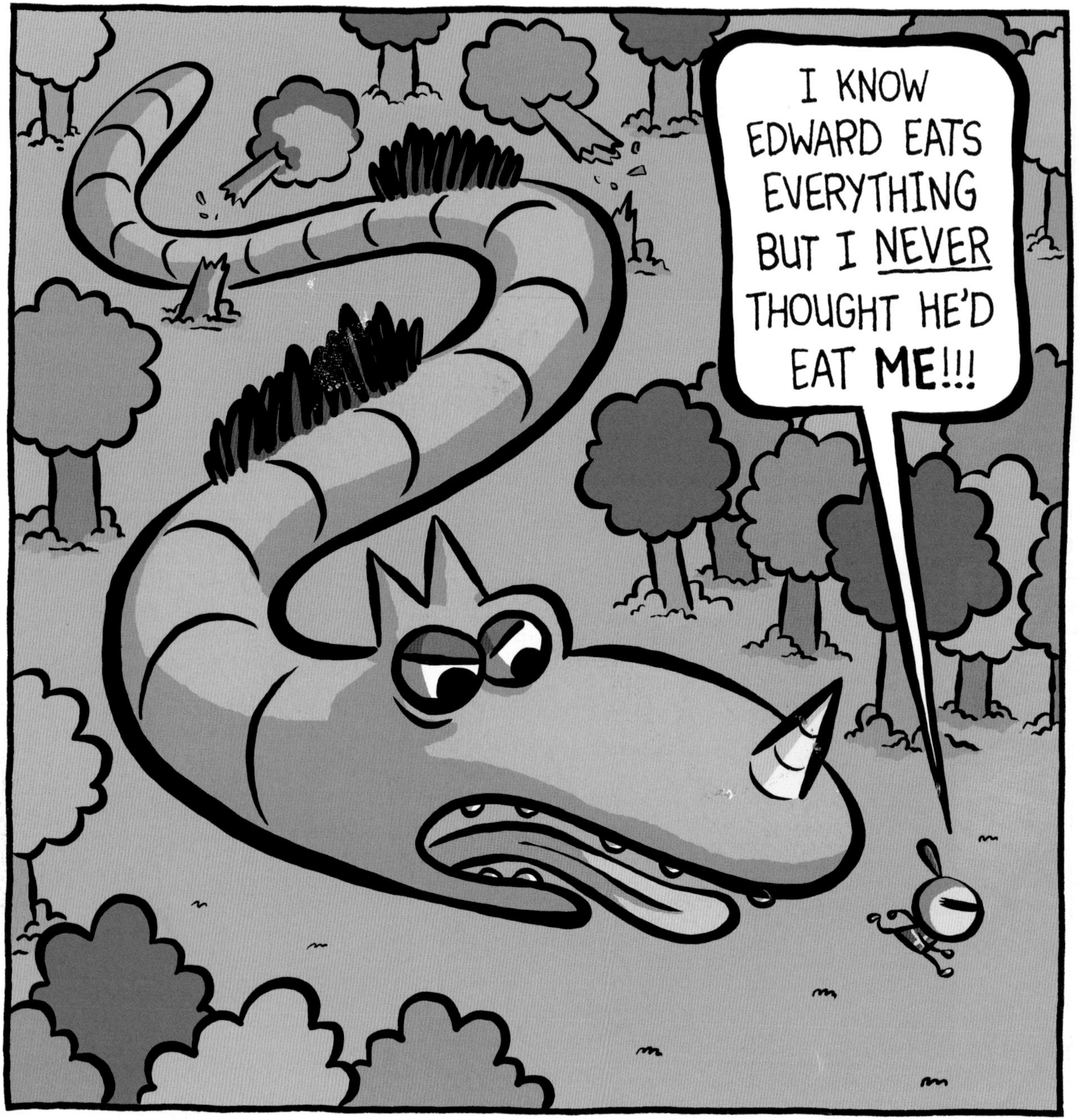
I KNOW EDWARD EATS EVERYTHING BUT I NEVER THOUGHT HE'D EAT **ME**!!!

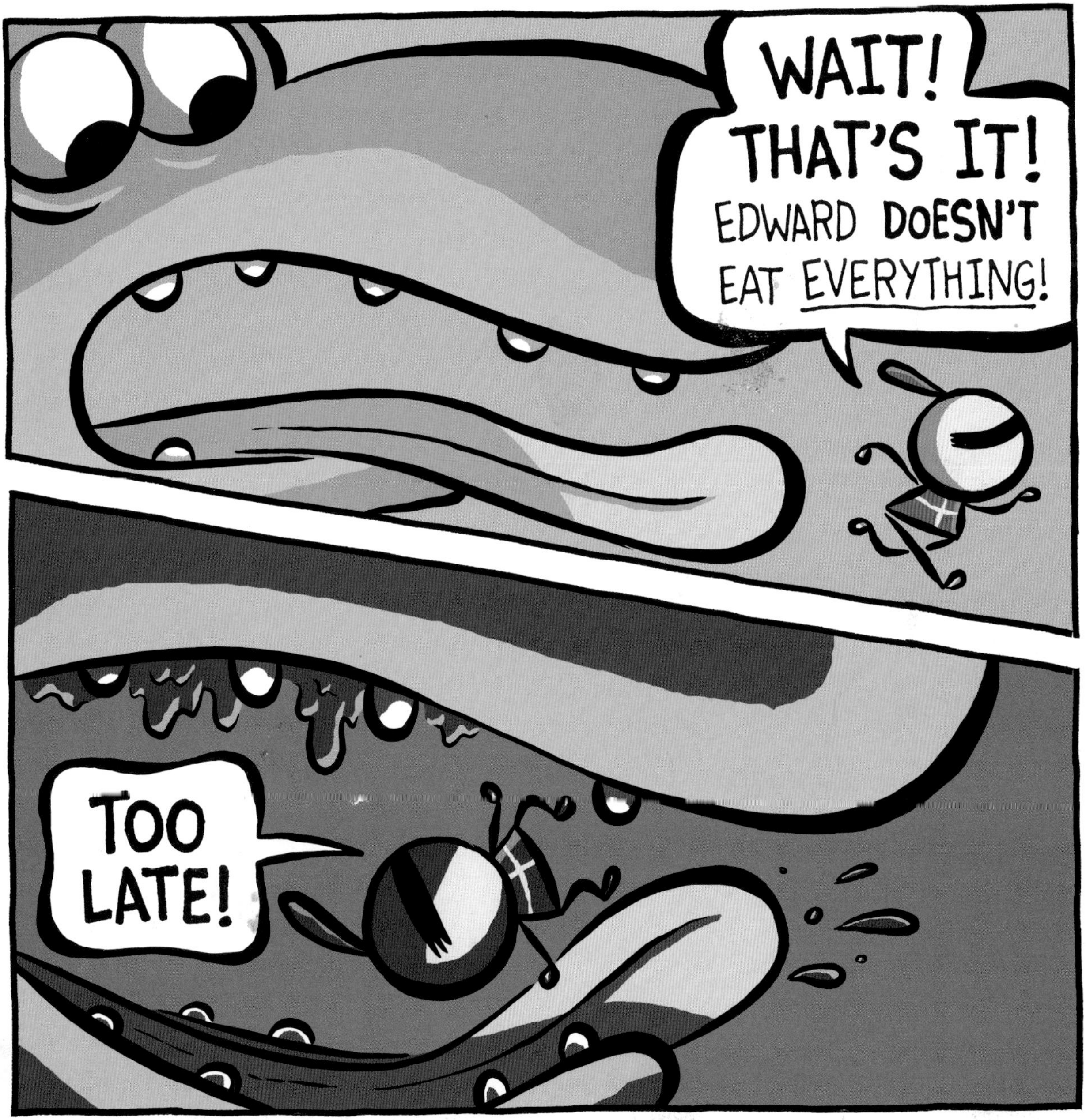
WAIT! THAT'S IT! EDWARD DOESN'T EAT EVERYTHING!
TOO LATE!

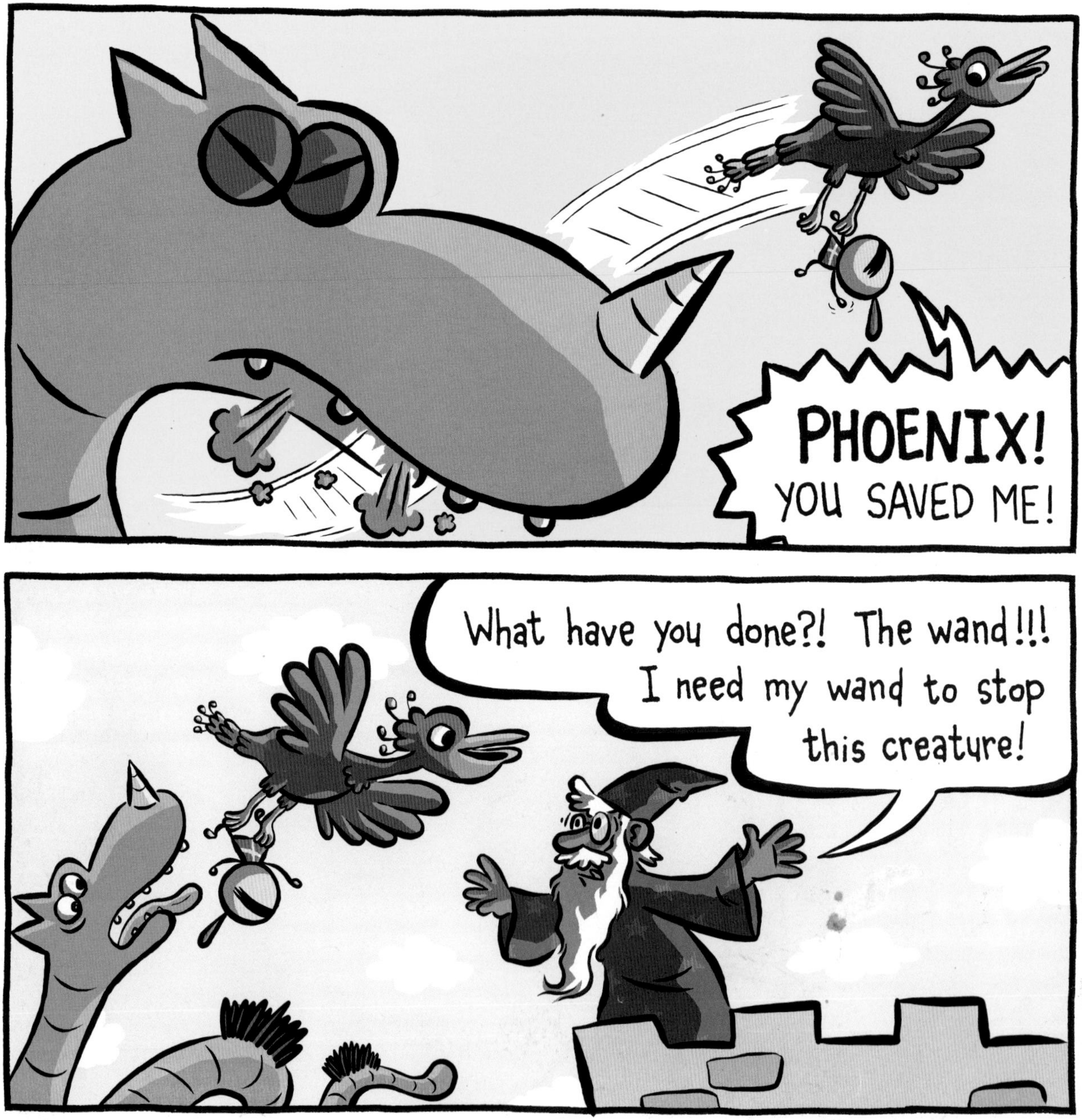
PHOENIX!
YOU SAVED ME!
What have you done?! The wand!!!
I need my wand to stop this creature!

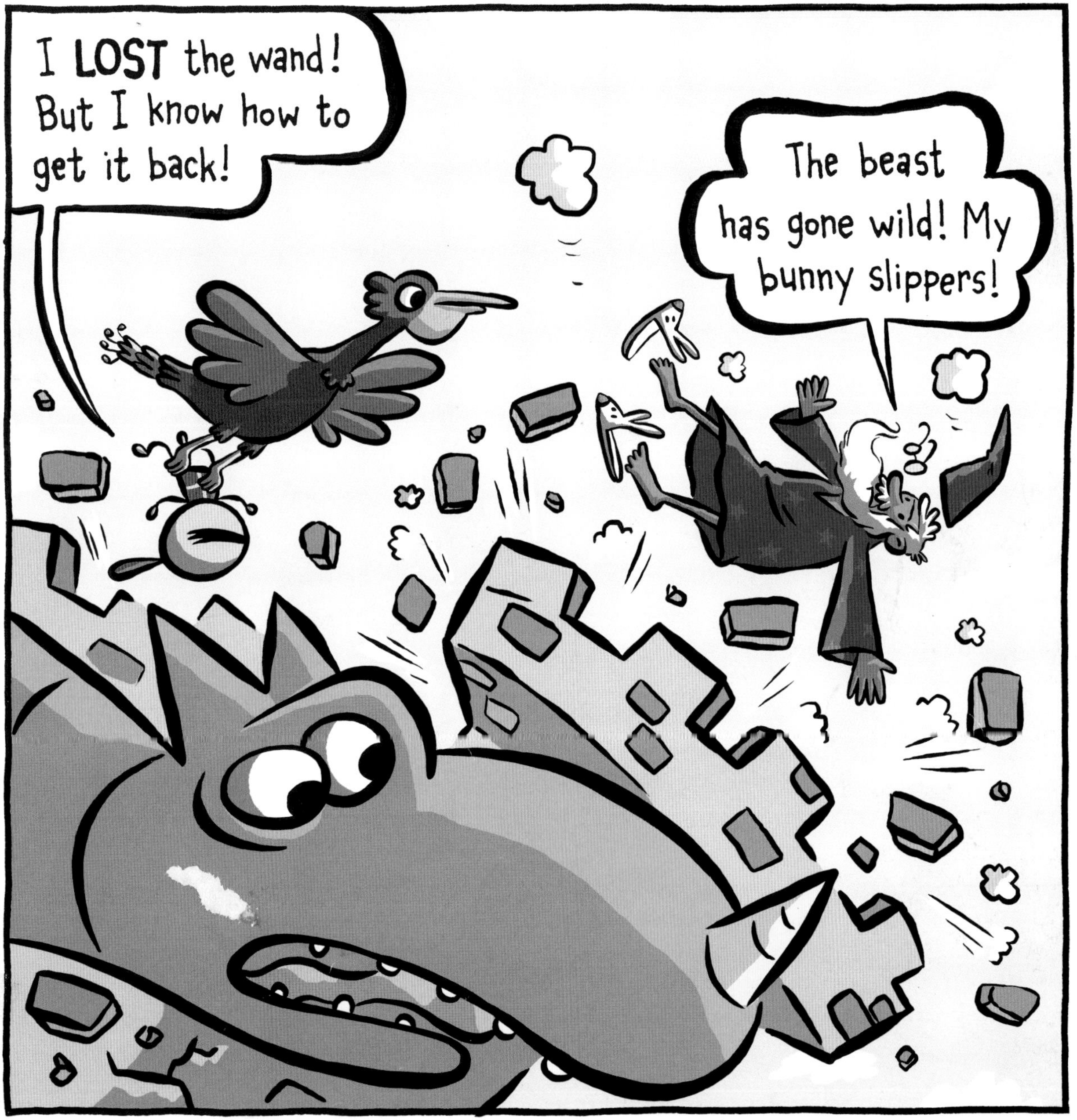
I **LOST** the wand! But I know how to get it back!
The beast has gone wild! My bunny slippers!

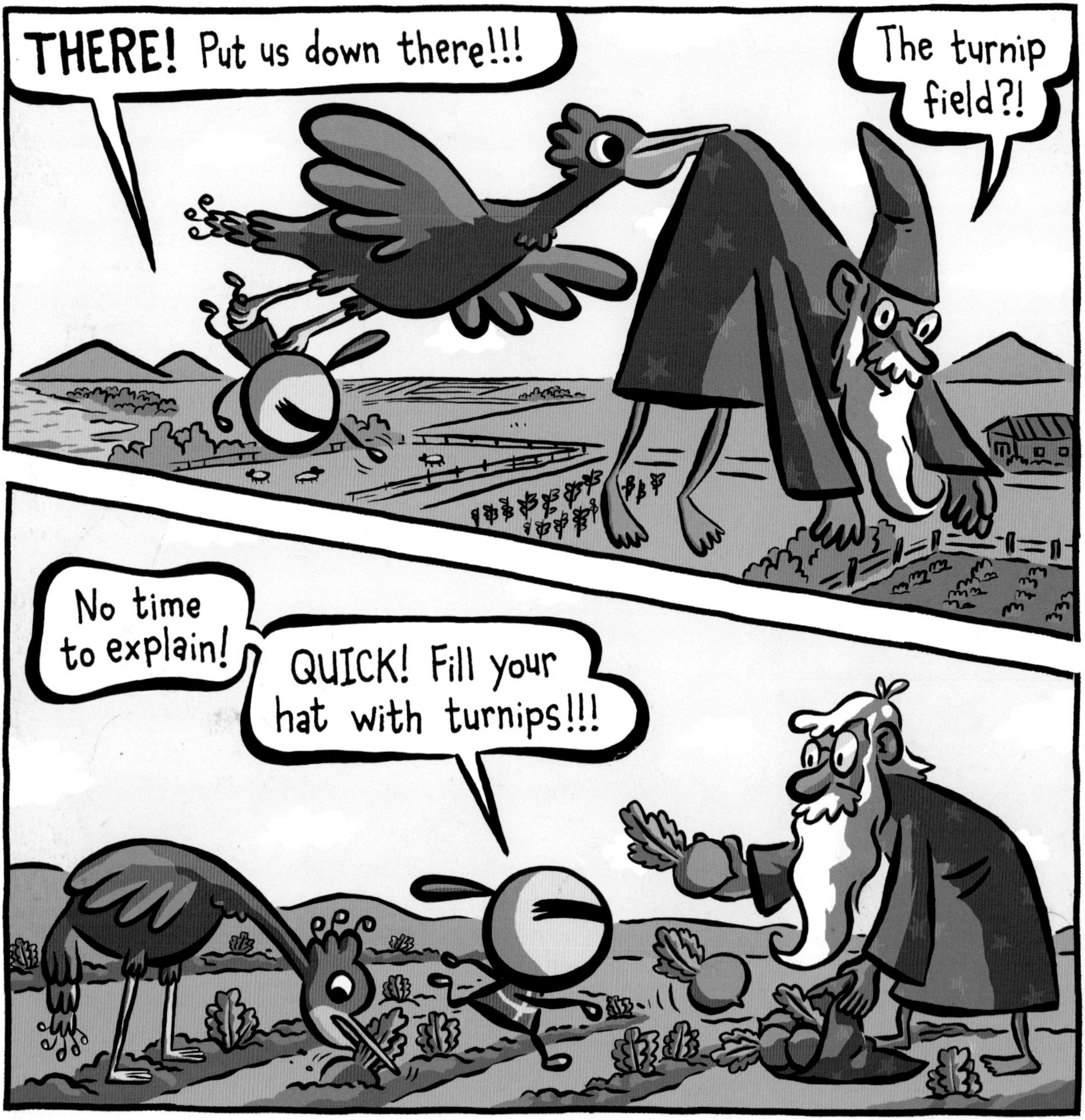
THERE! Put us down there!!!
The turnip field?!
No time to explain!
QUICK! Fill your hat with turnips!!!

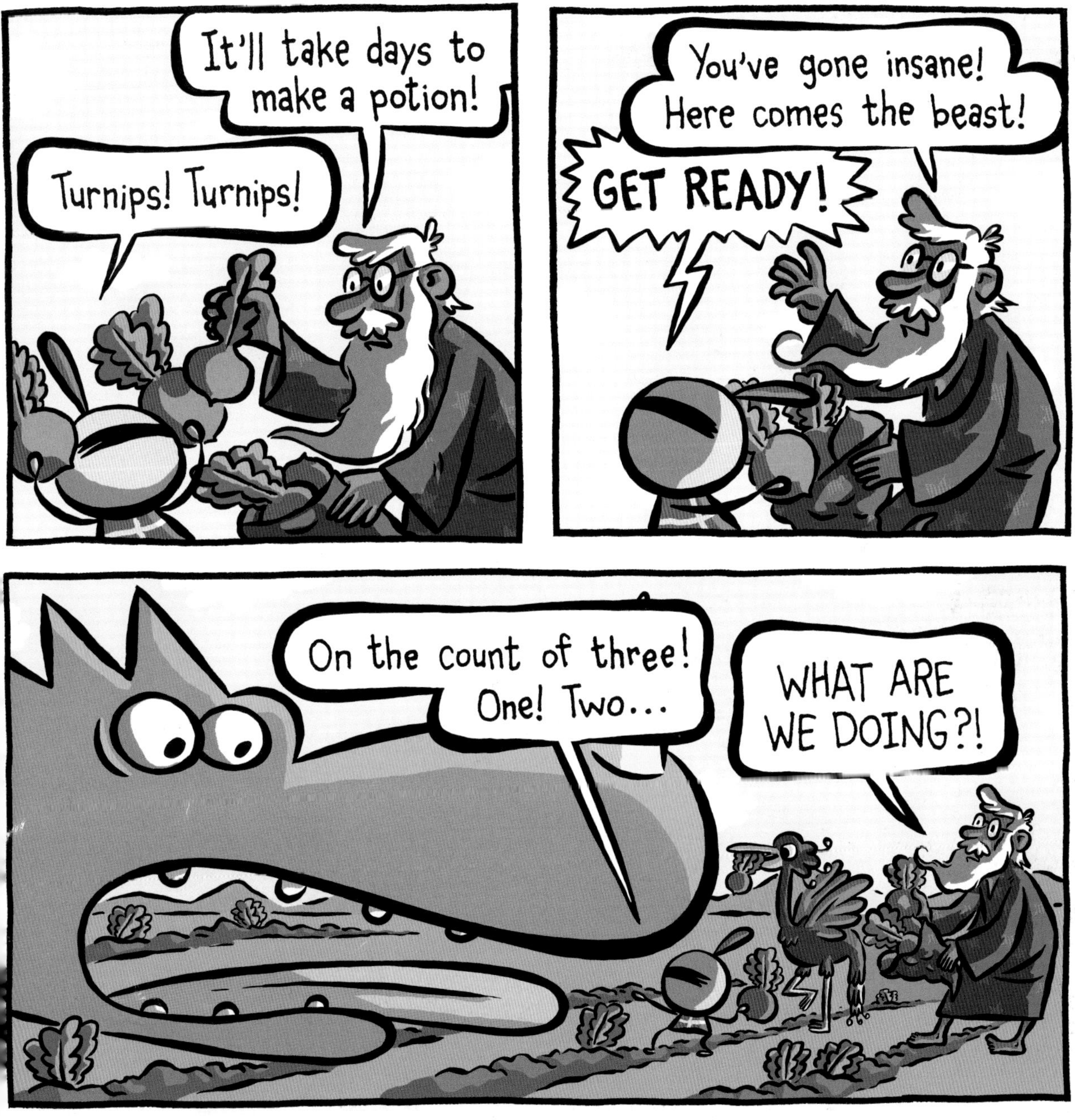
It'll take days to make a potion!
Turnips! Turnips!
You've gone insane! Here comes the beast!
GET READY!
On the count of three! One! Two...
WHAT ARE WE DOING?!

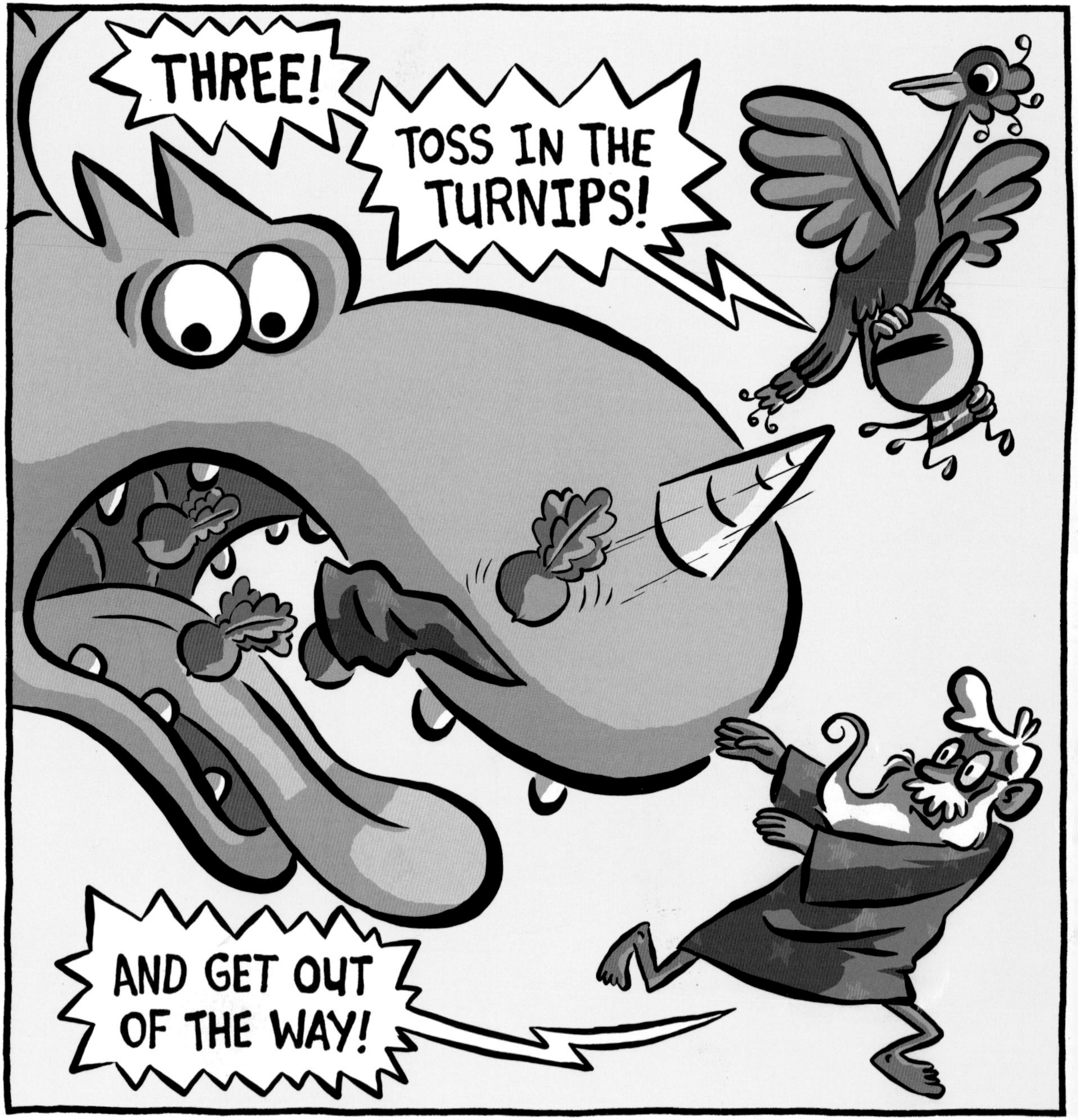
THREE!
TOSS IN THE TURNIPS!
AND GET OUT OF THE WAY!

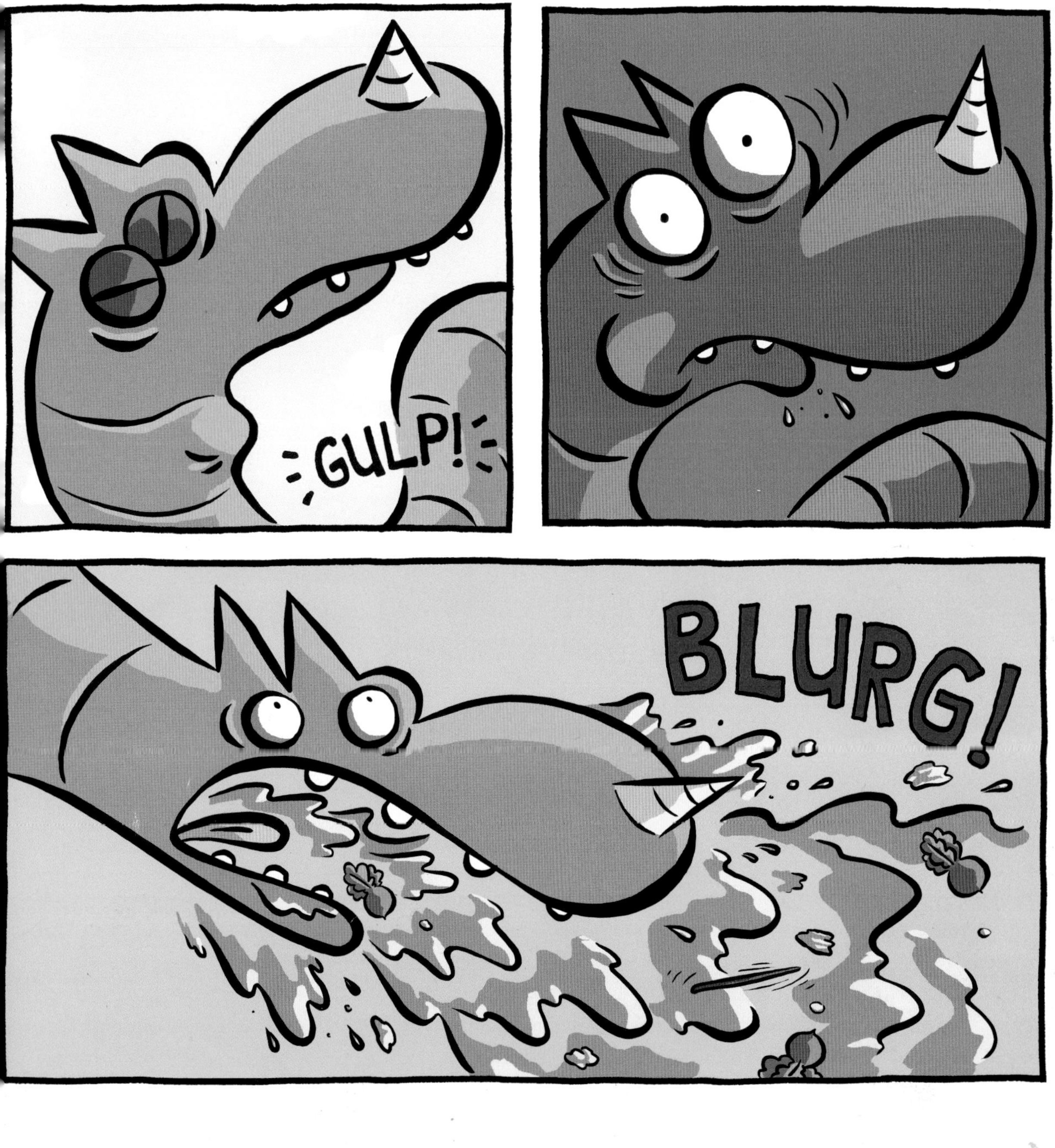
GULP!
BLURG!

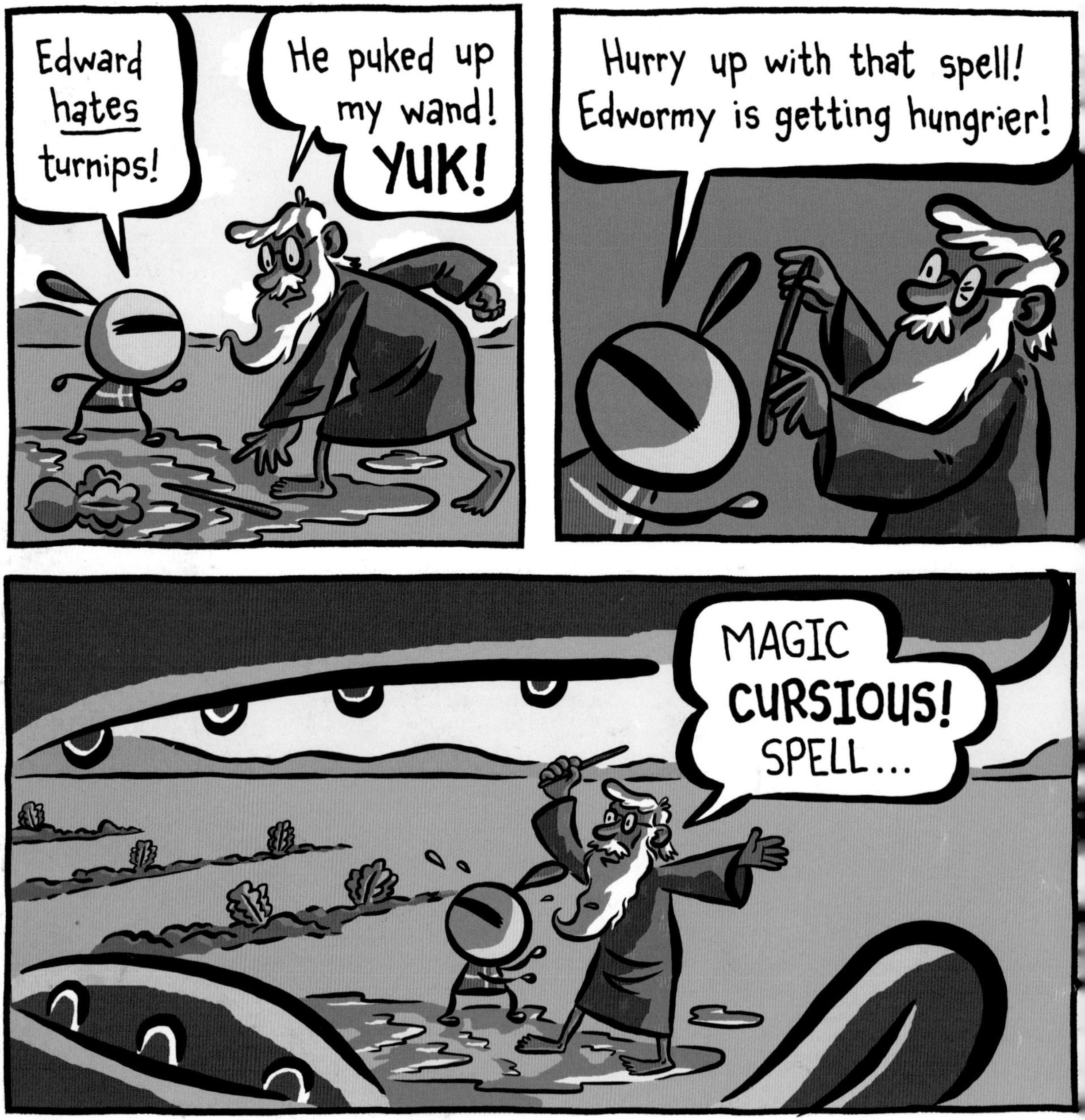
Edward hates turnips!
He puked up my wand! YUK!
Hurry up with that spell! Edwormy is getting hungrier!
MAGIC CURSIOUS! SPELL...

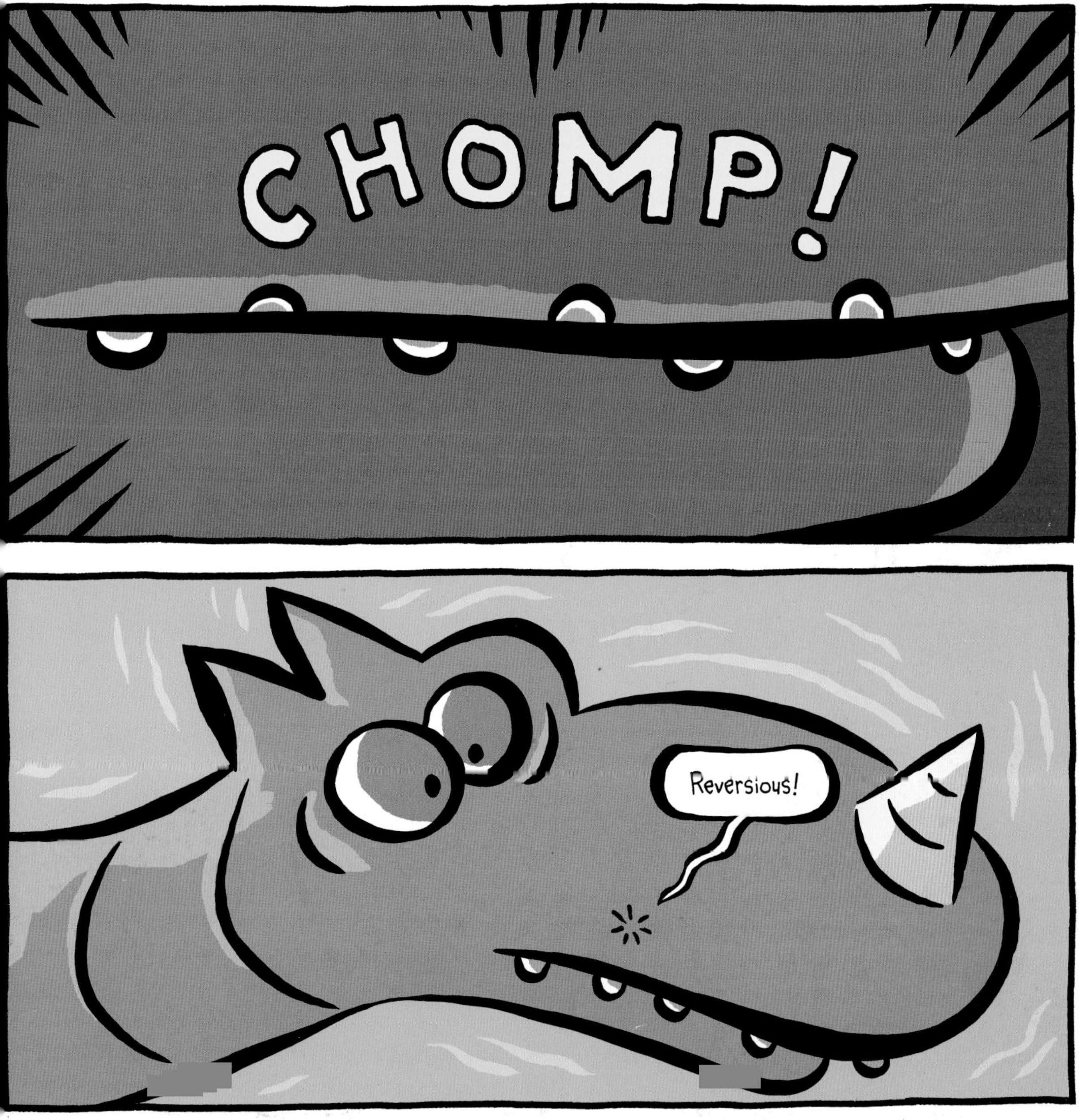
CHOMP!
Reversious!

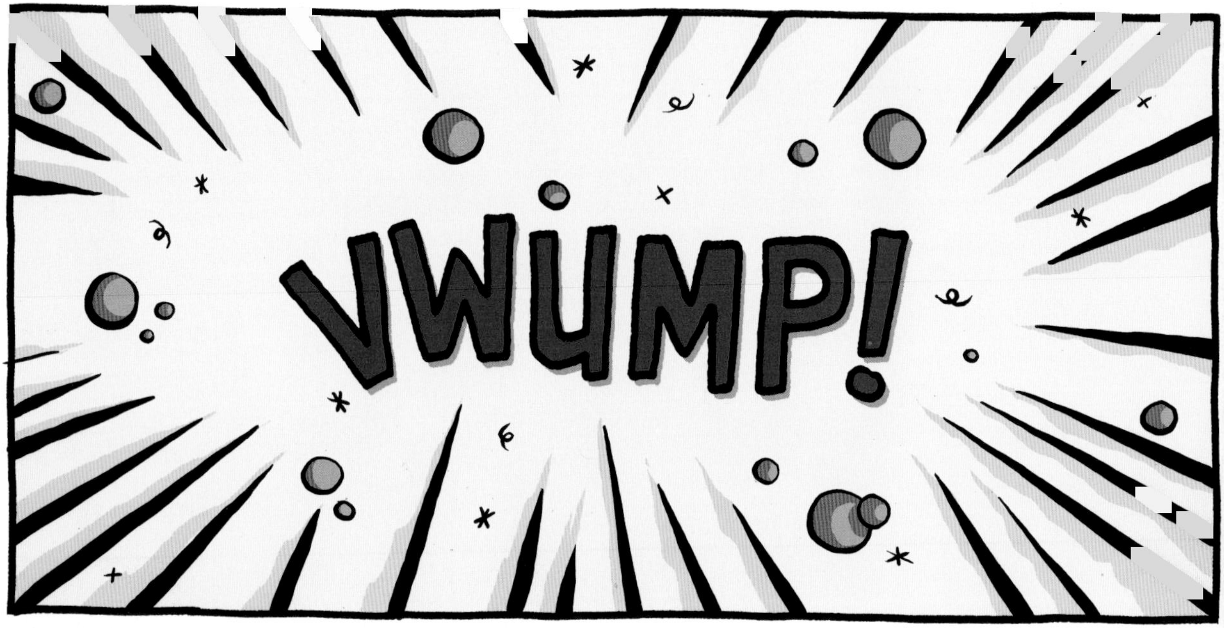
VWUMP!

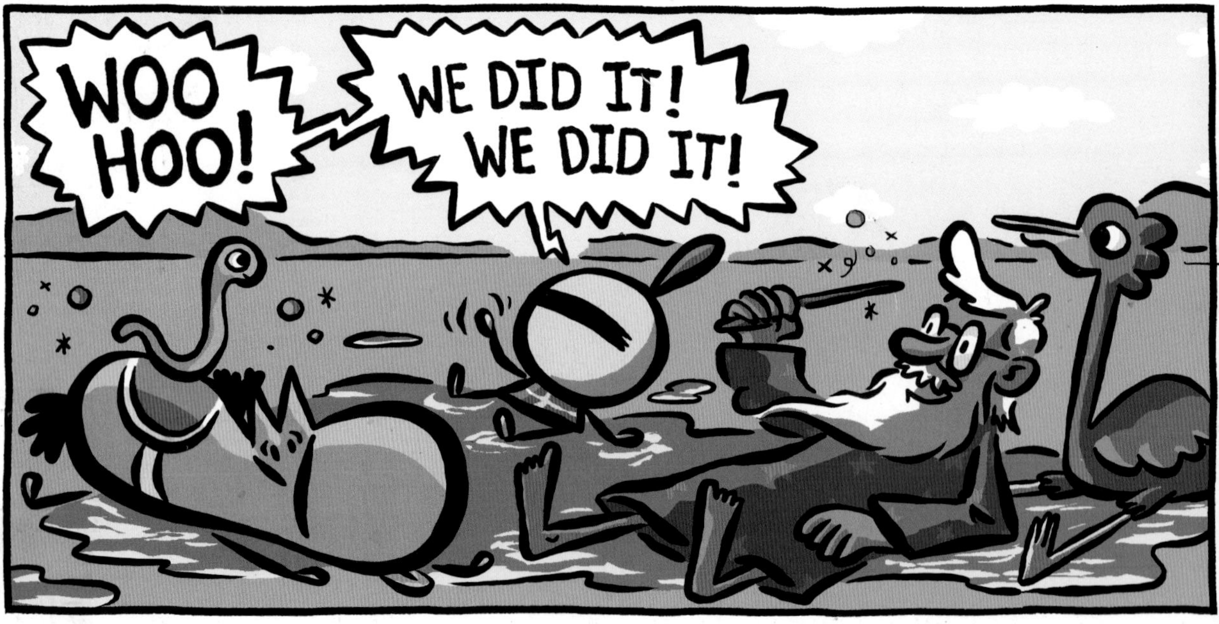
WOO HOO!
WE DID IT! WE DID IT!

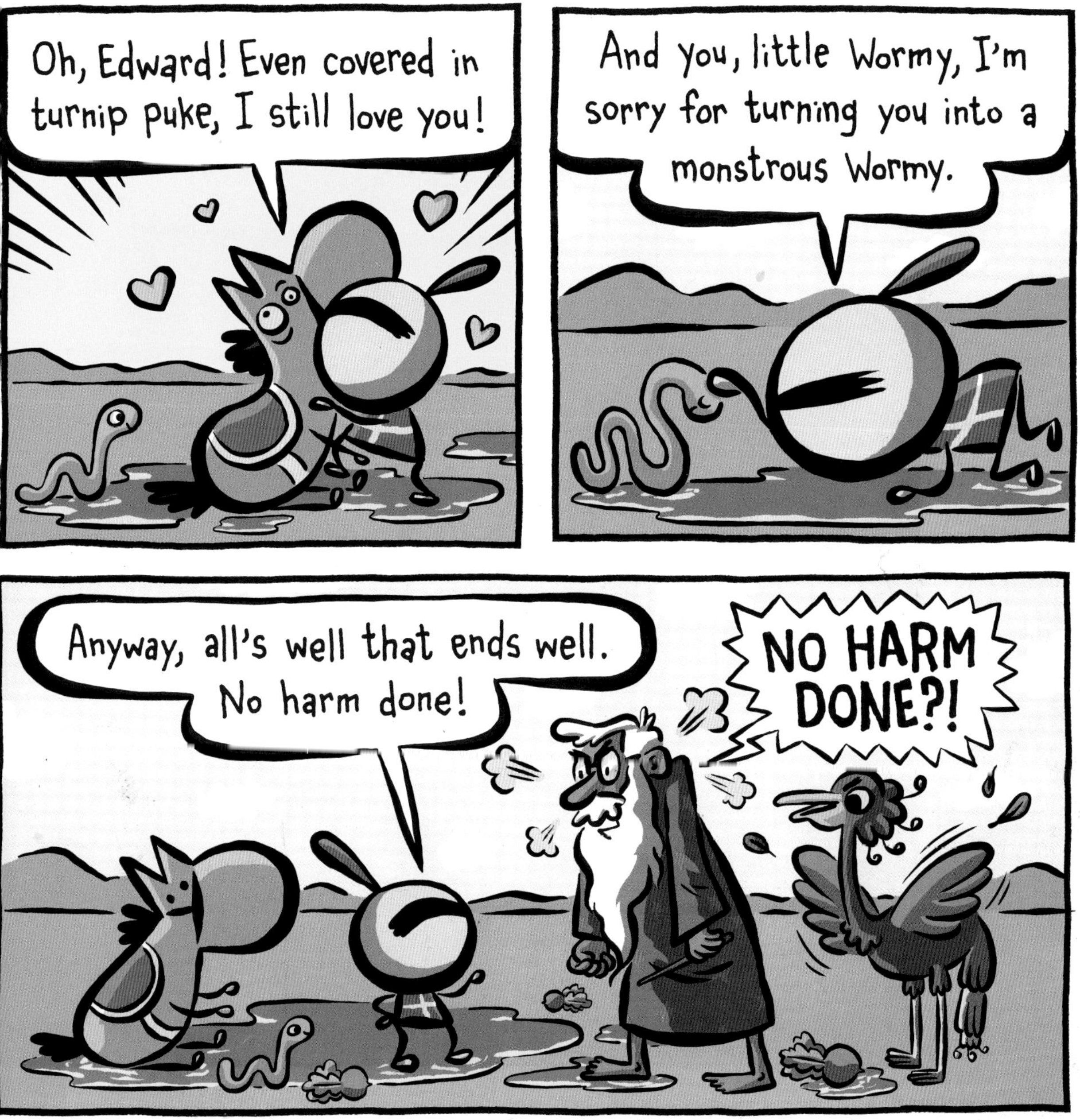
Oh, Edward! Even covered in turnip puke, I still love you!
And you, little Wormy, I'm sorry for turning you into a monstrous Wormy.
Anyway, all's well that ends well. No harm done!
NO HARM DONE?!

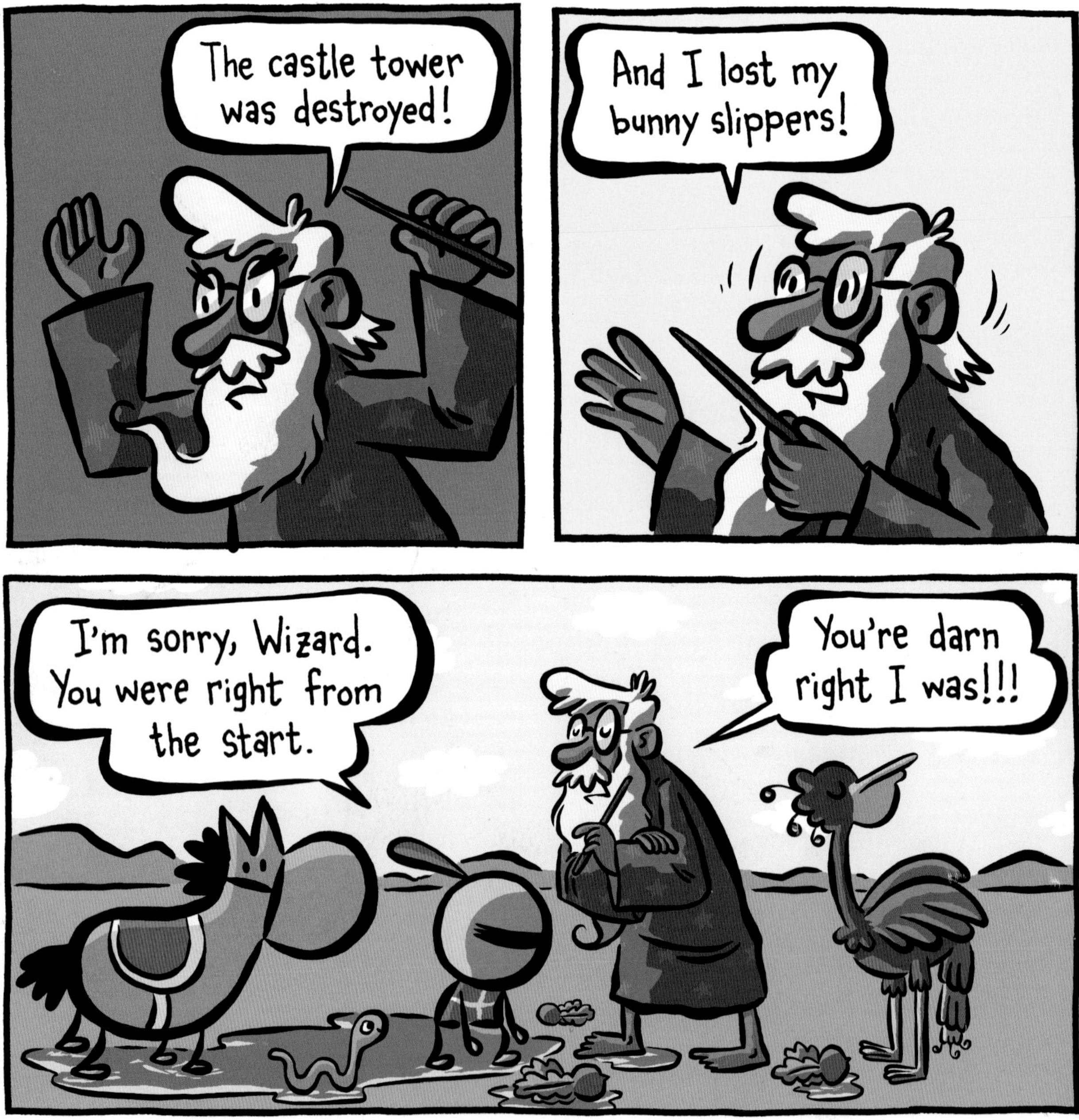
The castle tower was destroyed!
And I lost my bunny slippers!
I'm sorry, Wizard. You were right from the start.
You're darn right I was!!!

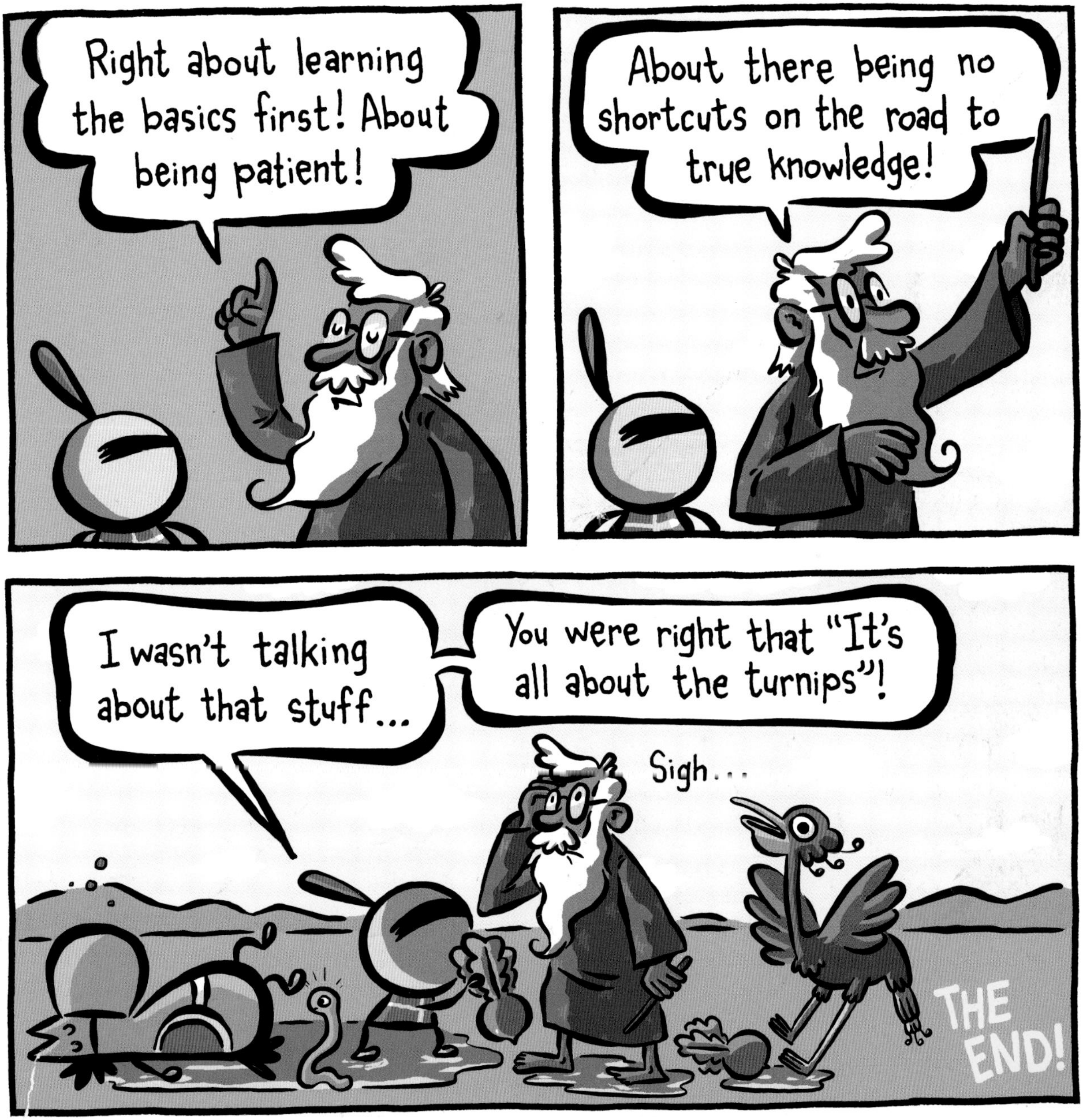
Right about learning the basics first! About being patient!
About there being no shortcuts on the road to true knowledge!
I wasn't talking about that stuff...
You were right that "It's all about the turnips"!
Sigh...
THE END!

First Second
New York

Published by First Second
First Second is an imprint of Roaring Brook Press, a division of
Holtzbrinck Publishing Holdings Limited Partnership
175 Fifth Avenue, New York, New York 10010

Library of Congress Control Number: 2016938209

ISBN: 978-1-59643-654-1

Our books may be purchased in bulk for promotional, educational, or business use.
Please contact your local bookseller or the Macmillan Corporate and Premium Sales Department
at (800) 221-7945 ext. 5422 or by email at MacmillanSpecialMarkets@macmillan.com.

FIRST EDITION

First edition 2017
Printed in China by Toppan Leefung Printing Ltd.,
Dongguan City, Guangdong Province

1 3 5 7 9 10 8 6 4 2

BY ART WE LIVE

HOCUS FOCUS was drawn and colored in Adobe Photoshop using a Wacom tablet.
Text was hand-lettered on Vellum paper using Staedtler pigment liner pens.

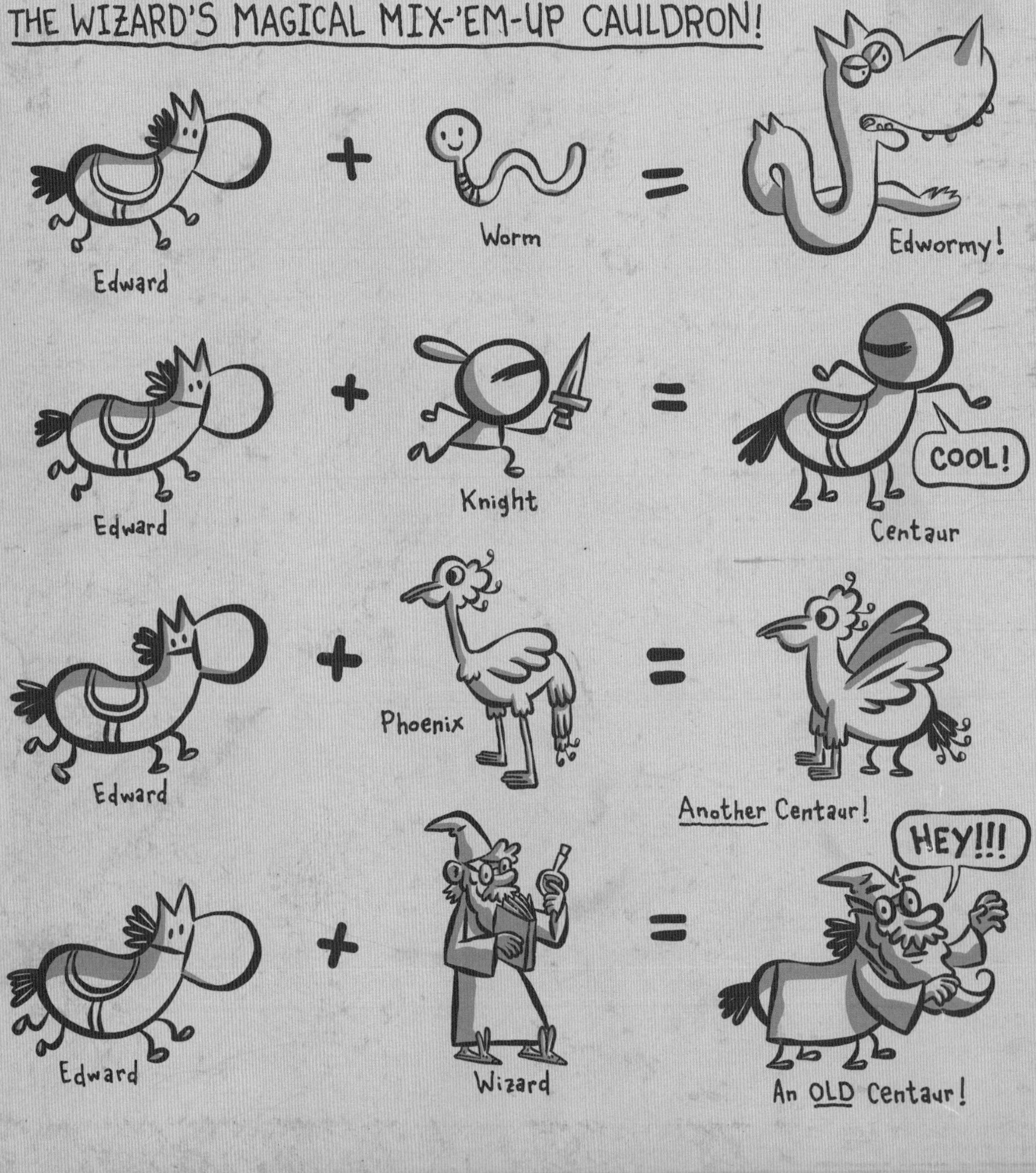
THE WIZARD'S MAGICAL MIX-'EM-UP CAULDRON!
Edward
+
Worm
=
Edwormy!
Edward
+
Knight
=
COOL!
Centaur
Edward
+
Phoenix
=
Another Centaur!
Edward
+
Wizard
=
HEY!!!
An OLD Centaur!